Christian Heroes: Then & Now

C. S. LEWIS

Master Storyteller

JANET & GEOFF BENGE

YWAM Publishing is the publishing ministry of Youth With A Mission (YWAM), an international missionary organization of Christians from many denominations dedicated to presenting Jesus Christ to this generation. To this end, YWAM has focused its efforts in three main areas: (1) training and equipping believers for their part in fulfilling the Great Commission (Matthew 28:19), (2) personal evangelism, and (3) mercy ministry (medical and relief work).

For a free catalog of books and materials, call (425) 771-1153 or (800) 922-2143. Visit us online at www.ywampublishing.com.

C. S. Lewis: Master Storyteller

Published by YWAM Publishing
a ministry of Youth With A Mission
P.O. Box 55787, Seattle, WA 98155-0787

Library of Congress Cataloging-in-Publication Data
Benge, Janet, 1958–
C. S. Lewis : master storyteller / by Janet and Geoff Benge.
p. cm. — (Christian heroes)
Includes bibliographical references (p.).
ISBN-13: 978-1-57658-385-2 (pbk.)
ISBN-10: 1-57658-385-6 (pbk.)
1. Lewis, C. S. (Clive Staples), 1898–1963—Juvenile literature.
2. Authors, English—20th century—Biography—Juvenile literature.
I. Benge, Geoff, 1954– II. Title.
PR6023.E926Z5858 2007
823'.912—dc22 2007006022

Third printing 2013

Printed in the United States of America

Christian Heroes: Then & Now

C.S. LEWIS

Master Storyteller

CHRISTIAN HEROES: THEN & NOW

Adoniram Judson
Amy Carmichael
Betty Greene
Brother Andrew
Cameron Townsend
Clarence Jones
Corrie ten Boom
Count Zinzendorf
C. S. Lewis
C. T. Studd
David Bussau
David Livingstone
Dietrich Bonhoeffer
D. L. Moody
Elisabeth Elliot
Eric Liddell
Florence Young
Francis Asbury
George Müller
Gladys Aylward
Hudson Taylor
Ida Scudder
Isobel Kuhn
Jacob DeShazer
Jim Elliot
John Wesley
John Williams
Jonathan Goforth
Lillian Trasher
Loren Cunningham
Lottie Moon
Mary Slessor
Nate Saint
Paul Brand
Rachel Saint
Rowland Bingham
Samuel Zwemer
Sundar Singh
Wilfred Grenfell
William Booth
William Carey

The British Isles

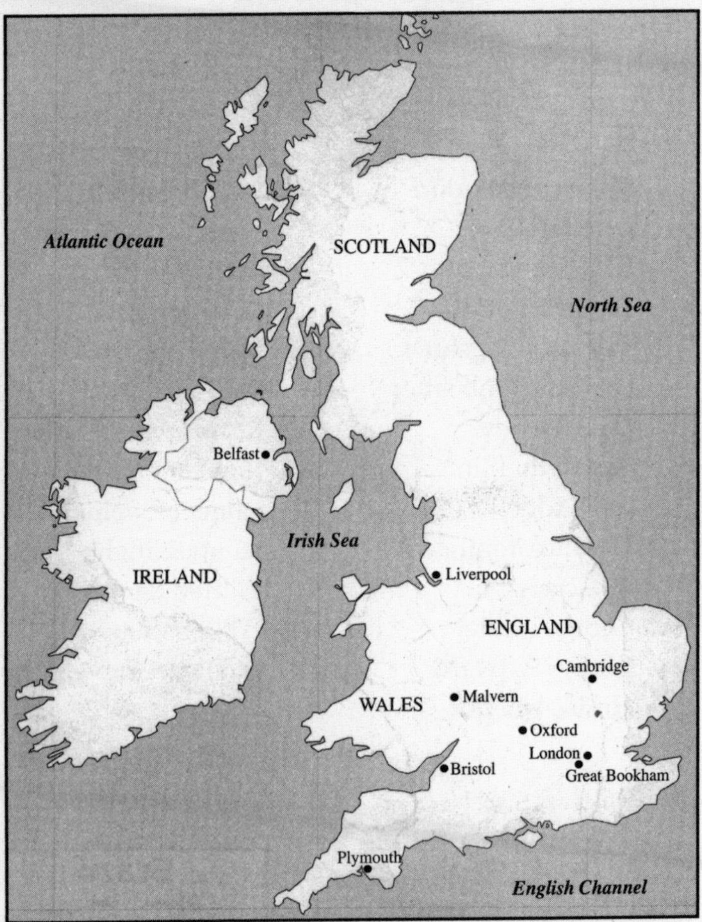

Contents

Chapter 1

A Lively Imagination

Clive Staples Lewis, who since he was two years old had insisted everyone call him Jack, stamped his foot hard in a puddle. Mud splattered all over his brother Warren's coat.

"What did ye have to do that for, Master Jack?" his nursemaid Lizzie Endicott asked, using his preferred name. "You've got the wee popes all over Warnie."

Jack, who was only six years old at the time, understood perfectly what Lizzie meant by "wee popes." Lizzie used the word *pope* to mean anything dirty or ugly—a constant reminder to everyone that the Roman Catholic Church and anything associated with it was an abomination. Probably the only place in the world where this language would make any sense at the time was in Ireland, where Jack was born on November 29, 1898.

At the turn of the twentieth century, Ireland was a country fiercely divided along religious lines. In the seventeenth century, Protestant England began to assert its dominance over Catholic Ireland. As part of this subjugation, English monarchs "gave" grants of Irish land to their favorite English lords. Many of these lords built elaborate castles and homes in Ireland, but they seldom lived there. Instead, they sent others to manage their land and send the profits from it back to England, thus becoming absentee landlords, while the native Irish languished in extreme poverty. As was to be expected, this situation created great animosity in Ireland, and one of the ways it showed itself was in Protestant hatred of Catholics—and in Catholic hatred of Protestants.

The Lewis family was a player in this historic struggle. Jack's grandfather, Richard Lewis, was a Welshman whose family had moved to England and then emigrated to Belfast, Ireland, to become part of the booming shipbuilding industry there. And Jack's mother's parents, Thomas and Mary Hamilton, both came from wealthy English Protestant families who had been granted Irish lands in the 1700s. Grandfather Thomas Hamilton was an Episcopal vicar at St. Mark's in the Belfast suburb of Dundela, and he took every opportunity to rail against Catholics from his pulpit. In fact, he often preached that Catholics were possessed by the devil.

None of this seemed to bother young Jack too much—he was much more interested in the stories of Ireland than in the religious struggles the country faced. And his nursemaid Lizzie was a constant source of such stories. Every night when she put Jack and Warren to bed, she told them some new tale from ancient Irish myths. There were tales of the famous seer-warrior Fionn MacCumhaill, who ate the "salmon of knowledge" to become wise and then fought giants and magicians as he made his way to a strange house, where he was told deep truths. And there was the champion Lugh, who slew his grandfather, a cruel man with a powerful eye that destroyed all it gazed upon.

Lizzie also told Jack that fairies were living in the mysterious dirt mounds around the outskirts of Belfast. Sometimes, she insisted, these fairies kidnapped people and brought them to their hidden palaces for nights of banqueting. Such tales fed Jack's young imagination. He loved to go for walks into the countryside, where he hoped to catch a glimpse of a fairy hurrying around the side of a hill.

Because Belfast was an unhealthy place, Jack's mother, Flora Lewis, was relieved that both her sons loved the countryside more than the city. An open sewer ran through Belfast, and damp fog lay over the city for days at a time. When Jack was born, the average life expectancy of a newborn in Belfast was nine years. As a result, concerned parents did all they could to keep their children from becoming infected with the prevailing diseases: diphtheria, whooping cough, cholera, scarlet fever, and especially typhoid, which had swept through Belfast the year before Jack's birth.

Flora was determined to do a more thorough job with her boys than most mothers. She banned her sons from going outside when it rained, which was about two hundred days a year. Instead, Jack and Warren were held behind a specially designed "gate" at the back door. The gate was a series of boards placed across the bottom of the door opening so that the boys could see the wet world beyond the house but not get wet themselves. In the middle of December, the darkest period of the year, when the sun set at 3:50 in the afternoon, the boys were allowed to play in the attic, which was illuminated by oil lamps. And each summer, Mrs. Lewis took her two sons, along with several servants, to holiday beside the sea. Their destination was always the same: Castlerock in County Down. Although the place was only fifty miles northwest of Belfast, getting there was one big adventure to the Lewis brothers.

The trip began with a horse-drawn cab ride to the train station in Belfast, followed by a leisurely train journey through the green countryside. Jack loved to travel in the front carriage of the train, and sometimes he even managed to persuade the engineer to allow him to climb up into the steam locomotive with him.

Once they arrived at Castlerock, the family would settle into a furnished house beside the sea, and then Flora would let her sons explore. Jack and Warren loved to leap from rock pool to rock pool, turning over seaweed in search of crabs and digging giant holes that were filled with water by the incoming tide. Although Warren was three and a half years older than Jack, the two brothers were best friends and hardly noticed the age difference between them.

Lizzie pointed out many places with special mystical powers. She also told Jack and Warren about leprechauns and how they hid a crock of gold at the end of every rainbow. Her story made quite an impression on both boys, who determined to find out whether this was true. An opportunity to do this came back in Belfast after a vacation. While out on a short walk one day, Jack looked up and saw a huge rainbow, which appeared to end right in the front garden of the Lewis house. He ran inside, grabbed a shovel, and persuaded Warren, who was a little more cautious, that they had to dig in the front yard to find the crock of gold the leprechauns had buried. The two boys dug furiously. By the time the sun went down, they had excavated a large hole, but, alas, they found no gold.

Later that night Albert Lewis arrived home, tired and irritated from his day's work as a government lawyer. Unwittingly he walked right into the large hole in the front yard and became convinced that his sons had created it as a booby trap for him. Although Jack tried to explain why he and Warren had dug the hole, his father would not believe a word he said. He was so furious with them that he punished each of the boys severely. This was a tough lesson for Jack to learn—not everyone could enter into his imaginary world and appreciate his efforts to prove whether or not it was true.

As soon as he learned to write, Jack began recording stories. There was the story of Sir Peter Mouse, the "knight in waiting" of King Bunny; and Sir Ben, a courageous frog. They all lived in Animal-Land in the fourteenth century and had many adventures, some of which Jack illustrated and made into crude books.

Jack liked to make things, too, as did Warren. A memory that was to stay with Jack all his life was of Warren presenting him with a tiny model garden. The garden had been assembled on a biscuit-tin lid with a pattern of moss, stones, and leaves that represented the wild Irish landscape. Jack was only six at the time, but the model created a strange surge of excitement in him, as if he had some memory of seeing it before. This feeling was something he would later come to call "joy."

Nothing much else exciting happened to Jack until he was seven years old. That was when his family and the servants moved into a new house. The Lewises employed five servants: a cook, a gardener, a governess, a nursemaid, and a housemaid. Jack's grandmother Lewis had died, and his grandfather wanted to come and live with the family, making the rented house in Belfast much too small for everyone to fit in comfortably. So Albert designed "Little Lea," a mansion on the outskirts of town. Or at least it seemed like a mansion to the two Lewis boys. The house, which was three stories high, was made of brick and had bay windows. The grounds were spacious and bordered on farmland so that the boys could walk or run in the fields.

From the window at the west end of the nursery in the new house, Jack and Warren had a wonderful view of the bustling Belfast shipyards on the Belfast

Lough. From there they could watch hundreds of ships and boats of all shapes and sizes navigating their way up and down the lough. The view gave both brothers endless hours of entertainment.

Beyond the lough to the north lay the green hills called the Glens of Antrim in County Antrim, and to the south, the Castlereagh Hills in County Down. They seemed so far off and mysterious to Jack, and he wondered what magical lands lay beyond them.

The best thing of all about the new house was the small attic rooms that ran the entire length of the house and were connected to each other by small doors. Together, the attic rooms formed a kind of narrow tunnel right under the roof tiles. The house was so big that the attic was not needed for storage, and since none of the adults had any particular interest in banging their heads against the low-hanging rafters, they never ventured up there. The attic was Jack and Warren's private domain. In one of the small rooms, trunks and suitcases were stacked; in another was a pile of old canvas and a mound of yellowing newspapers. In still another was a wobbly, three-legged table. The boys stocked this room with pencils, chalk, paint boxes, and all sorts of paper and set to work creating their own world. Jack created the imaginary country of Boxen, drawing and painting pictures of it and its inhabitants, as well as writing stories about the place. Meanwhile Warren created a fantasy India in his mind that he, too, drew and wrote about.

The boys' adventures in their fantasy worlds were cut short, however, a month after the family moved into Little Lea. Warren, at ten years of age, was sent off to school in England. This was not unusual; many Anglo-Irish families sent their sons off to get a good education in England. But few of them sent their sons off to a place as hell-like as Wynyard House School in Watford, Hertfordshire. It sounded like a good school from the literature Mr. and Mrs. Lewis had read about the place, but in fact it was a very abusive place. Jack, though, would not learn of the true horrors of the school until years later, when he too was sent off to Wynyard House.

Meanwhile Jack found life at home dull without Warren. His father insisted that he spend more time downstairs. Every evening after dinner, Jack, his mother, and his father would all retire to the library, where they read for several hours. Jack was allowed to read any of the hundreds of books in the house, and he soon grew to love animal stories like *Black Beauty* and magical stories by Edith Nesbit, a prolific children's author. Jack was particularly entranced by her book *The Story of the Amulet*, which described how some children in London stumbled upon a magic amulet that could transport them back in time to fabulous lands.

During the day, a governess named Miss Harper tutored Jack. However, it was Flora Lewis, herself a graduate in mathematics from Queen's College, Belfast, who insisted on teaching Jack French, Latin, and math. These were the lessons Jack enjoyed the most. During this time Jack grew to admire his mother's wit and intelligence.

In the afternoons, when his lessons were over, Jack would climb upstairs to the attic and continue making up his own stories. He also wrote letters to Warren keeping him informed as to what was going on in Boxen. "At present Boxen is SLIGHTLY CONVULSED," he wrote in one letter. "The news has just reached her that King Bunny is a prisoner. The colonists (who are of course the war party) are in a bad way: they dare scarcely leave their houses because of the mobs. In Tararo the Prussians and Boxonians are at fearful odds against each other and the natives. General Quicksteppe is making plans for the rescue of King Bunny."

To Jack's delight, during the summer of 1907, Mrs. Lewis decided that instead of Warren coming home to visit, she and Jack would collect Warren in London and the three of them would vacation on the northern coast of France. This was eight-year-old Jack's first time out of Ireland, and he enjoyed every minute of the trip. In London they visited the zoo, where Jack saw elephants and zebras, though he was most taken with a cage of white mice.

From London, Flora and her sons crossed the English Channel and made their way to the seaside village of Beneval, near Dieppe. Reunited, Jack and Warren enjoyed exploring the village and the seashore. And inspired by his trip to the zoo in London, Jack started writing a book he titled *Living Races of Mouse Land.*

Back in Belfast for another year without Warren, Jack continued reading many of the books in the Lewis house. He read *Paradise Lost* and decided he needed to spend time reflecting on what it was about. He was also spurred on to write more, and he produced a wide variety of books that he inventoried on a sheet of paper, titled "List of My Books":

Building of the Promenade (a tale)
Man Against Man (a novel)
Town (an essay)
Relief of Murray (a history)
Bunny (a paper)
Home Rule (an essay)
My Life (a journal)

Jack had started keeping his journal at Christmas, just after his ninth birthday. In it he wrote a description of his servants and family. "I have a lot of enymays [enemies] however there are only 2 in this house they are called Maude and Mat. Maude is far worse than Mat but she thinks she is a saint. . . . Papy [father]," Jack went on to explain, "is the master of the house, and a man in whom you can see strong Lewis features, bad temper, very sensible, nice when not in a temper." His mother, Mamy, he wrote, is "like most middle aged ladys, stout, brown hair, spectacles, knitting is her chief industry." Jack then turned the attention on himself. "I am like most boys of nine, and I am like Papy, bad temper, thick lips, thin and generally wearing a jersey." Grandfather Lewis, who had moved into Little Lea after Jack's grandmother died, is also described. He is "a nice old man in some ways." But he indulged in self-pity, and Jack notes, "However all old people do that."

Jack's simple and predictable life changed in February 1908. Suddenly the adults in the house began whispering among themselves and exchanging knowing looks. Over the years Jack had grown accustomed to his mother's being unwell, as she suffered from asthma and headaches. But this time she was sick with something much worse. The doctor diagnosed it as stomach cancer and ordered that she have an operation immediately.

Jack looked to the adults in his life for assurance that everything would be all right with his mother, but no one thought to speak to him about what might lie ahead for his mother and the whole Lewis family.

Chapter 2

Big Changes

On February 15, 1908, Flora Lewis underwent surgery for stomach cancer right in her own bed in her bedroom. Three doctors and two nurses came to the house and transformed the upstairs into a makeshift hospital ward. Jack retreated into the attic while he waited to hear whether or not his mother would survive the operation. As the smell of ether and disinfectant wafted up through the ceiling into the attic, he wondered what would happen to him if his mother died. It was hard for him to imagine. Family pets had died before—a dog, a canary, and two mice. But what was it like when a parent died? Jack had no idea.

Much to his relief, Jack did not have to find out what it would be like. His mother survived the operation and regained her strength. However, a death did occur in the Lewis family. Two months after his mother's operation, Jack's grandfather Lewis, who had lived with them at the Little Lea house since the family moved into it, had a stroke and died.

Following Grandfather Lewis's death, Jack's father became withdrawn and moody, so much so that Jack found it difficult to have a conversation with him. And soon after Grandfather Lewis's funeral, Flora's health began to decline, and Jack's mother grew weaker by the day. This situation made Jack's father even more moody, until Jack hated being in the same room with him.

Although Flora's father was an Episcopal minister, the Lewis family was not particularly religious. They attended service every Sunday at St. Mark's Church, where Jack read aloud from the prayer book and recited psalms, but no one talked much about God in the home. Still, nine-year-old Jack was determined to pray until his mother was healed. Every morning he got up and said prayers for her, begging God to reverse her illness and make her well again. But it was to no avail.

On July 8 Jack realized how serious things must be, because Warren was brought home from school in England to say goodbye to their mother. Neither brother knew what to do, and they both tried to keep as quiet as possible and stay out of the way of the adults in the house. They retreated upstairs to the attic and entered their alternate worlds of Boxen and India. During this time Jack worked at linking these two worlds. He wrote a story about King Bublich II, who inhabited his imaginary world, and about how the king had discovered "India." Jack also painted a map of his world in which India was not a country in Asia but a large island off the coast of Animal-Land. And Warren mapped the sea routes between the two kingdoms and drew pictures of the vessels that traveled those routes.

August 23, 1908, was Albert Lewis's forty-fifth birthday, but there was no celebrating at Little Lea that day. Early in the morning while Jack was still in bed, his father came into the room. "Your mother has gone," he said.

Jack struggled to wake up properly and take in what his father had just said. Gone where? To see a doctor? To the seaside? Then the horrible truth crept over him—not gone somewhere but gone forever!

Soon both brothers were dressed in their Sunday-best clothes and led into their parents' bedroom.

"Look at her. Isn't she beautiful?" one of their aunts asked.

Jack wanted to vomit. His mother lay fully dressed on top of the bed. As far as he could see, there was nothing beautiful about his mother's dead body. He was not looking at "her"; he was looking at "it."

The funeral and burial that followed were a blur in Jack's mind as he tried to grasp what had happened to him and, just as important, what would happen to him now. His father behaved strangely, sobbing uncontrollably sometimes and at other times telling the boys to leave the room because he did not want to see them.

Things only got worse when Jack's uncle Joseph, his father's older brother, died unexpectedly ten days after Flora's death. There was another round of family visitors, with the now familiar journey to the church in the hearse for the funeral service and burial in St. Mark's churchyard.

Jack and Warren waited for things to return to normal at Little Lea, though deep in his heart, Jack knew they never would. Jack's father was barely able to function after the death of his father, his wife, and his brother in a four-month period.

Jack always assumed that he would eventually follow in his brother's footsteps to school in England, but now his father seemed desperate to get rid of him. As a result Jack was enrolled at Wynyard House School in Hertfordshire with Warren, and hasty preparations were made for the boys' departure for England.

Within three weeks of his mother's death, Jack found himself walking along a Belfast quay in the evening. The three Lewis men, Jack, Warren, and their father, walked in awkward silence as Jack's new boots made a hollow sound on the wooden dock. Every step he took irritated Jack. He had never worn such uncomfortable clothes before, and the thought of spending the next four years dressed in them was almost more than he could bear. He wore a bowler hat that perched on his head. The hat was slightly on the small side and fit with a vicelike grip. Jack also wore an Eton collar—a large, white starched affair that chafed at his neck—a tightly buttoned waistcoat, and knickerbockers.

The three of them found their way to the ship that would ferry the boys to England and clambered up the gangplank. It should have been an exciting moment, but it reminded Jack of the happy summer voyage he had taken with his mother to England and France in what now appeared to him to have been a different and more innocent life.

Eventually, with a great sigh of relief, Albert Lewis announced that the ship would be leaving soon and he had better disembark. Then he burst into a bout of sobbing. Both brothers looked on stoically. Jack, for one, had seen enough adult shows of emotion in the past few months to last him a lifetime, and he was glad when his father composed himself and turned and left the ship.

As bleak as the situation was, Jack and Warren managed to exchange smiles as the ship cast off from the quay. With a belch of black smoke from the ship's funnel, the propeller began to churn the water, and the vessel started its journey down the Belfast Lough to the open sea. Jack stood on the starboard side of the ship and peered into the night, hoping to catch a last glimpse of a light from the Little Lea house. But all he saw was darkness.

The following morning the ship docked in Liverpool, where the boys disembarked and made their way to the train station. As the train rattled its way closer to London, Jack's confusion and grief hardened itself into an instant dislike of England. Jack compared the flimsy wooden fences to the sturdy stone walls of Ireland, and the imposing redbrick farmhouses to the picturesque white cottages of home. Even the shape of the haystacks annoyed him—the stacks were taller and more pointed than Irish haystacks.

During his times at home, Warren had said little about life at Wynyard House, and Jack found himself wondering why he did not have more information about their destination. He would find out soon enough.

The brothers changed trains at Euston Station in London for the twenty-minute ride to Watford. Jack took a deep breath as he stood outside his new school—an ugly, semi-detached, yellow-brick house with a strip of gravel in place of a garden and front yard. Inside the place was even grimmer than the outside. The dormitory where the nine boarders slept was stark and unwelcoming. The windows had no curtains, and Jack passed the first night with a full moon shining in his face.

The following day, school lessons began as Jack struggled to grasp the full extent of the misfortune that had befallen him. The headmaster of Wynyard House School, the Reverend Robert Capron, ruled the place like a mad sea captain. The morning began with breakfast in the dining room. The boys, nine boarders and eight day boys, sat at one end of a long table. At the other end of the table sat the Reverend Capron with his silent wife, his son, whom the boys named Wee Wee, and his three sullen adult daughters. Wee Wee appeared to be the only person who had the courage to speak to his father, and then only when replying to a question.

The boys ate in silence, and each spoonful of porridge felt like a lump in Jack's mouth, so much so that Jack could barely swallow. Already, just one day into his school experience, Jack dreaded what would come next.

Following breakfast the boys were all marched into a single schoolroom. The walls held no charts or other interesting reference tools, just three canes lined up on hooks and ready to be pulled down and applied to a boy's legs or bottom at any time.

Arithmetic was the first lesson, though there was no formal instruction. The Reverend Capron, whom the boys nicknamed "Oldie," merely told the boys to start writing sums on their slates. Oldie did not seem to care what the sums were. The exercise lasted for two hours, and Jack began to wonder whether he was ever going to be taught anything.

A short break followed arithmetic, and then it was time for the boys to study Latin. Here again Oldie barely spoke, and Jack found himself going over the Latin exercises he had learned from his mother. He could almost hear her voice, reading along with him, gently correcting him. It was all he could do to keep from crying.

Lunch proved to be as dismal as breakfast, and after lunch the boys were sent outside to exercise, which consisted of playing a game of rounders on the gravel strip at the front of the school building. As Jack ran around on the sharp stones, he wished for the soft, green grass that surrounded Little Lea.

Jack soon learned to hate any form of organized sports, mainly because he and Warren had inherited defective thumbs from their father. A normal thumb has two joints that bend, but the Lewis brothers each had only one bending joint on each of their thumbs, making them clumsy at holding a bat or catching a ball.

Afternoon studies were just as boring and undirected as those in the morning, though Jack did get his first glimpse at how Oldie disciplined his students. During class, Oldie asked one of the boys, Peter, a question regarding a geometrical proof. Peter began to give his answer, but it was not correct. Jack watched in shock as Oldie pulled down one of the canes from the wall and began beating the desk yelling, "Think! Think! Think!" at Peter.

Despite the admonishment to think, a clearly frightened Peter could not come up with the right answer.

"Come here, boy," Oldie finally demanded.

Jack watched as Peter gingerly walked forward.

"Bend over there," Oldie said, pointing to a spot at the front of the classroom.

Peter did as he was commanded while Oldie walked to the back of the room with his cane in hand. Suddenly Oldie spun around, ran forward, and brought the full weight of the cane down as hard as he could against Peter's backside. Peter made no sound as Oldie turned around and repeated the procedure. Six times he stroked the cane against Peter's bottom, and when Oldie was done, Peter let out a whimpering groan of pain that made Jack feel sick to his stomach. It was one the worst acts of cruelty Jack had witnessed, and he decided, as much as he was able, to try to avoid being punished with the cane.

The living conditions at Wynyard House also shocked Jack. Back home at Little Lea he was used to having the run of the house, but here every move had to be accounted for. There was one washroom with a single tub, and each boy got to take a bath once a week. The toilet situation would have been enough to get the school closed had it ever been inspected. There was only one outhouse, located at the back of the school, and no one ever cleaned it. To make matters worse, the boys' snacks and any extra food sent to them from home were stored in the outhouse.

The situation at Wynyard House did not improve, and each day Oldie seemed to make up new rules and new punishments to go with them. Two weeks after arriving there, Jack wrote a pleading letter home to his father.

> My dear Papy,
>
> Mr. Capron said something I am not likely to forget—"Curse the boy" (behind Warnie's back) because Warnie did not bring his jam to tea, no one ever heard such a rule before. Please may we not leave on Saturday? We simply CANNOT wait in this hole until the end of term . . .
>
> Your loving son Jack.

Unfortunately Albert did not respond to his son's plea, and the Lewis boys were left at Wynyard to fend for themselves until the end of term.

The only bright spot during this time was that Oldie often banished the boys from school and commanded them to go for long walks together. Sometimes the boys were told to go out for the entire day. Instead of walking for miles, the boys stopped at nearby villages and bought candies to sustain themselves. Then they would follow a canal as it meandered through the flat countryside. Trains and the odd motorcar raced by, adding to the general excitement. It was on one of these walks that Jack enjoyed his first philosophical discussion. He and one of the older boys got into a conversation about whether the future was a line that had already been drawn or was rather an unknown entity that was created at the time it happened. Jack loved the conversation and realized that he much preferred talking about ideas than about everyday matters, like school.

When the Lewis boys returned to Little Lea for Christmas, Jack was sure he could convince his father not to send them back to Wynyard House School. But Mr. Lewis turned a deaf ear to his pleas, convinced that a little hardship would go a long way to toughening his boys up in the English school tradition. And so the boys returned to Wynyard House School.

That year, 1909, in which he turned eleven years old, Jack had begun to find solace in Christianity. As a young boy in Ireland, religion had been all around him. His grandfather Hamilton was a preacher, who recited an endless number of psalms to himself as he turned senile, and his mother had liked to read the Church of England prayer book. Jack, however, had never thought about the personal implications of Christianity until his time at Wynyard House. The experience of school there was so bad that Jack found himself looking forward to the Sunday visit to St. John's Church for the morning service.

At first Jack had been put off by the High Church feel of St. John's, where the members of the congregation crossed themselves and bowed to the altar. But soon this subsided, and Jack began to listen to the sermons and prayers, and he decided to do everything he could to be a good Christian.

Jack took to praying each night and morning and reading his Bible every day. The practice helped him bear his times at school a little more easily, as did his visits home to Ireland, where Jack and Warren liked nothing better than to pack a picnic lunch and bicycle off into the countryside of County Down. By then cars were becoming more common on Irish roads, and Warren was fascinated with them. But for his part, Jack preferred to stay out of their way, often hopping over a fence when he heard a car coming toward him.

After Jack had been at Wynyard House School for one year, Warren graduated and went on to study at Malvern College in rural Worcestershire. In Jack's mind this provided the perfect opportunity for him to leave the school as well. But Jack's father would have none of it. Still wrapped in his own grief at the death of his wife, father, and brother, he had no idea how bad things had become at Wynyard. In fact the situation had become so bad in 1909 that another parent had complained of abuse to the police and a scandal had followed. The matter was settled out of court, but half of the remaining students were withdrawn from the school, leaving just four day boys and five boarders, one of whom, unfortunately, was Jack Lewis.

After the police investigation, Oldie became even more erratic. He prowled the hallway looking for boys to punish and took to holding the shorter boys up high by their collars and swinging the cane at their calves. The effect reminded Jack of a macabre pendulum on a grandfather clock. Fortunately Jack, who was a good and quiet student, managed to avoid being beaten himself, but he suffered terribly watching his friends being so cruelly treated. Within a year of Warren's leaving Wynyard House School, Oldie was a broken man, unable to carry on the daily affairs of running even the smallest of schools. One day he announced that Wynyard was closing and he was going back to his vocation as a minister.

Jack was astonished that his prayers had been answered. Wynyard House School was over—it was history. But what lay ahead of him now?

Chapter 3

New Schools, New Trials

About a mile from the Little Lea house in Belfast, a redbrick school named Campbell College dominated the landscape. Even though the school was within walking distance of the Lewis home, Albert Lewis had not thought it appropriate for his sons to attend there. This was because he wanted Warren and Jack to be able to fit into English upper-class society, something that would be difficult to achieve if they mixed with Irish boys in an Irish school instead of English boys in an English school. Still, in a moment of weakness, and faced with the imminent closure of Wynyard House School, Mr. Lewis agreed that Jack could return to Belfast and enroll at Campbell College. The only thing he insisted upon was that Jack be a boarder at the school rather than a day boy. And he agreed to sign a pass so that Jack could come home to visit on Sunday afternoons. At this stage Jack was glad to accept any kind of compromise that would keep him from having to attend another English school like Wynyard.

From the first day at Campbell College, Jack found it difficult to feel at home there. This was because as a junior student he had no place of his own except a bed and a locker. When school was out, he and the other boys wandered the great halls and lingered at the dinner table. Jack later described the experience as being like living in a railway station—and just like a railway station, all sorts of things went on there.

There was little institutionalized bullying at the school, but from time to time gangs of about ten or twelve boys would form and come up with some crazy stunt they would pull for as long as they could get away with it. Then they would fade back into the general school population. About a week after entering Campbell College, Jack found himself the victim of one of these gangs. One minute he was standing in a corridor, and the next minute five boys were charging at him. They caught him and dragged him headlong through a series of corridors until he had completely lost his bearings. Then they entered a dingy, low-ceilinged room. In the dim light Jack could make out four other young students like himself. The boys nodded to each other and awaited their fate in silence.

The boy to the right of Jack was the first to be hauled to his feet by the gang of bullies. The bullies pushed the boy's head down to his feet, and then they shoved the boy under a pipe that ran around the room about three feet above the floor. Suddenly, unexplainably, the victim was gone—disappeared into thin air—and then everything was silent. Chills went up and down Jack's spine as he tried to work out what had happened to the boy.

Two more boys suffered the same fate—whatever it was—and then it was Jack's turn to be dragged to his feet. Like those who had gone before him, he was bent in two and pushed under the pipe. He found his body pushing against a trapdoor that gave way, and then he found himself tumbling downward. He landed with a thud on top of the boy who had gone before him. Once Jack regained his senses, he realized that the boys had all been dispensed to the coal cellar. Moments later another boy came barreling down the chute, and then the boys heard the sound of the trapdoor being bolted.

The boys sat together in the dark for what seemed like an eternity until they heard the rattling of the padlock and the trapdoor was opened. One by one the boys crawled up the chute and back into the low-ceilinged room. Their captors had fled, and the boys all started laughing when they saw the sooty state of their faces and clothes. One of the boys led the rest back to the main hall, where they were all reprimanded for getting their clothes dirty.

Even though it was scary at the time, Jack did not find the episode troubling. He had heard of much more sinister things happening to new boys attending other schools.

Jack never got the opportunity to be anything but a new boy at Campbell College. He had barely begun to settle in when he came down with a serious case of bronchitis and was sent home to his father. At first Jack was disappointed to be leaving Campbell College, but as his health improved a little, he came to love the solitude of home. His father went off to work each day, leaving him to read, write, and draw for as long as he wanted. And Warren was not there to concoct trouble with. For the first time since his mother's death, Jack felt at ease around his father.

During this time Jack particularly enjoyed reading fairy tales and epic poems. His English teacher at Campbell College had introduced him to the work of Matthew Arnold, and Jack fell under the spell of Arnold's classic poem *Sohrab and Rustum.* With books as his friends and with his father's company at night, Jack could have stayed at home forever, but Albert Lewis had other plans. This time they did not involve Jack's going back to Campbell College. Instead, the plans were to send Jack to a small English boarding school located near Malvern College, which Warren was still attending.

In January 1911, after Christmas break, Jack and Warren once again set off together for England. Surprisingly, Jack did not have the same negative reaction to England as before, and he looked forward to seeing his new home. The school was called Cherbourg, and Jack loved it from the first time he saw it. It was nestled in the Worcestershire Hills near the town of Great Malvern, in western England near the Welsh border. With its mineral wells, Great Malvern had a reputation for being a place of healing waters. Because of this, many famous people came to town to "take the water cure," and a very un-English-looking community had sprung up there. The houses, which clung to the sides of the hills, looked like Swiss mountain houses, and gardeners took great care to trim the evergreen trees into fanciful shapes.

In his first letter home to his father, Jack wrote, "Malvern is one of the nicest English towns I have ever seen yet. The hills are beautiful but of course not so nice as ours."

The whole effect on Jack was magical, and he felt he had entered another world. But once he was enrolled at Cherbourg and assigned to his dormitory, things became less magical and more mundane. Again Jack found himself in a small school, with only seventeen students. The standard of teaching, however, was much higher. Not surprisingly, Jack's favorite activity was walking alone in the forest around the school.

Meanwhile, Warren was not setting a high example at nearby Malvern College. He hated Greek and Latin and soon devised a way to trade his English expertise for free papers in those subjects. Before long Warren and his group of friends had quite an enterprise going, each one doing all the homework in his area of strength and then sharing it with the other boys. Jack, on the other hand, loved all his subjects, apart from mathematics. He enjoyed translating works from classical languages and reading metaphysical papers.

Despite his academic success, Jack floundered about socially. He had not improved any in sports and found the other boys' preoccupation with cricket and rugby baffling. He struggled to figure out how to fit in. He began to worry about his looks and became anxious about girls. Behind a brave front, he was a shy, gifted young teenager looking for a place to belong.

The matron of the school, Mrs. Cowrie, soon picked up on this and went out of her way to become Jack's special friend and comforter. Unfortunately, this relationship ended disastrously when Jack set about to campaign for the right to send letters home without first having them approved by the headmaster. Mrs. Cowrie took Jack's side in the argument, and she was fired as a result.

The incident devastated Jack and took away the best friend he had at Cherbourg. Still, Jack had no choice but to plod on, and eventually he made friends with other boys who had interests similar to his.

Christmas and summer holidays continued to be the highlight of the year for Jack, though there was now a lot of tension at home between Warren and their father. Mr. Lewis accused Warren of being lazy and wasting his schooling. Warren fired back that his father lived the most boring life imaginable and if that was what years of scholarship got you, he did not want it.

The situation with Warren's schooling came to a head when Warren was caught smoking on the school grounds. He was not expelled immediately, but he was asked not to return to Malvern College for the fall term of 1913. Albert was furious about the situation. He felt that it was his responsibility to set both his sons on the right path to a useful career.

Following the summer holidays in Belfast in 1913, both boys returned once again to England. This time Warren had a new destination. He went to stay with Professor William Kirkpatrick in Surrey. W. T. Kirkpatrick, or "Old Knock," as he was known, had been Albert Lewis's headmaster many years before. Professor Kirkpatrick was a taskmaster and a stickler for routine.

It was a new start for both boys, since Jack had graduated from Cherbourg and won a classical entrance scholarship to Malvern College.

Jack knew what to expect when he got to Malvern, as he had lived in the shadow of the college for the past two years and had been there on numerous occasions to watch sporting events. His plan was to keep out of trouble and hope that no one took too much notice of him. His plan backfired from the start.

Each student at Malvern College was assigned to a club where he was to participate in compulsory games. Instead of checking for himself what club he was in, Jack relied on the information given to him by one of the older students in the school, a boy with the nickname Fribble. "You are in the same club as me, B6," Fribble said. Armed with this information

Jack went dutifully to the notice board to see which sports team he had been assigned to play on. To his delight, each week he learned that he had not been assigned to any team and thus did not have to participate in sports. *Perhaps Warnie told them how bad I am at sports,* he rationalized. But during his third week at school, Jack learned that Fribble had lied to him. He had not been assigned to the B6 club but was assigned to another club, and he had already failed to show up for several compulsory events. The punishment for this, whether the infraction was deliberate or not, was flogging with a cane by one of the school prefects. Jack accepted his punishment and vowed never to accept secondhand information again when he could just as easily get the information firsthand.

Fribble belonged to the most privileged group within Malvern College called the Bloods. A Blood was a student who had won the admiration of the rest of the college through his sports prowess and leadership. All the junior boys in the school wanted to grow up to become Bloods, mainly because of a system in the school called "fagging." Under this system a Blood was entitled to get any junior boy to do manual tasks for him. Jack and the other new arrivals at Malvern College soon found themselves with little free time. As soon as a Blood shouted, the students were all expected to report to him to see what he wanted. One or more boys would be assigned to menial tasks, such as tidying his study or cleaning his boots. Jack soon learned that the trick was to do an adequate job—well enough that you did not get a flogging for slacking on the job but not so well that you became the Blood's most conscientious worker, and therefore his favorite.

Jack did his best to fit in to what was going on around him. He feigned interest in sports, completed the tasks the Bloods gave him without complaining, and even pretended to pay attention at the twice-weekly church services. In fact, the religious fervor that Jack had felt in his younger years had by now drained from him. Jack told himself that he no longer believed in God and that Christianity was just another myth devised to keep the unhappy masses from giving up hope. He wrote to a neighbor in Belfast:

> How dreary it all is! I could make some shift to put up with the work, and discomfort, and the school feeding: such inconveniences can only be expected. But what irritates me more than anything else is the absolute lack of appreciation of anything like music or books which prevails among the people whom I am forced to call my companions. Can you imagine what it is like to live for twelve weeks among boys whose thoughts never rise above the dull daily round of cricket and work and eating?

By Christmas 1913, Jack had given up hope of ever really fitting in at Malvern College. When Warren came to meet him for the journey home to Belfast, Jack hoped that he would never set foot in the school again. He knew what he had to do—over Christmas break he had to convince his father to withdraw him and enroll him in another school somewhere else.

Chapter 4

"Old Knock"

Back in Belfast during Christmas break, Jack and his father struck a bargain. Jack would return to Malvern College for one more term, and then he could finish his schooling with William Kirkpatrick, "Old Knock," who had been tutoring Warren. It was a compromise he could live with, and Jack returned to Malvern College after Christmas to count down the days until he left the place for good.

At the same time, Warren entered the Royal Military Academy at Sandhurst in England as an officer cadet. With Warren being away from the influence of other boys at Malvern College, his academic work had flourished, and he had managed to win a cadetship at Sandhurst. He was ranked twenty-first out of the 201 young men who were accepted for the spring intake. It was a feat that astonished everyone and gave Albert Lewis great confidence in Professor Kirkpatrick's ability to tutor Jack as well.

During his last term at Malvern College, Jack spent most of his time in the school library. His English teacher suggested he read the poetry of Irish poet William Butler Yeats and the books *Northern Antiquities* by Paul Henri Mallet and *Myths of the Norsemen* by Hélène Adeline Guerber. Once he had read the books, Jack began writing his own northern tragedy, which he called *Loki Bound*. The story was about a boy who rebelled against his bloodthirsty, cruel father.

The term flew by, and in the summer of 1914, Jack packed his belongings and left Malvern College for good. His boarding-school days were over.

While 1914 was marked by the arrival of personal freedom for Jack, it was not so for Warren and many other young Englishmen. Europe was on the brink of war. On June 28, 1914, news reverberated around the world that a Serbian nationalist in Sarajevo had assassinated Archduke Franz Ferdinand, heir to the Austro-Hungarian throne.

Three weeks later the Austro-Hungarian Empire delivered an ultimatum to Serbia to hand over the assassin. The ultimatum escalated the conflict, with Russia standing behind Serbia, and Germany siding with the Austro-Hungarians. Europe, it seemed, was drifting closer to war with each passing day. Finally, on July 28, 1914, the Austro-Hungarian Empire declared war on Serbia. It was a sobering time for everyone in Europe and Great Britain. People waited anxiously to see whether the British would become embroiled in the war.

During the summer holidays, Jack tried to put these looming uncertainties out of his mind. He continued writing *Loki Bound* and much to his delight found someone to share it with. Jack had known the boy next door, Arthur Greeves, since the Lewis family moved into Little Lea. However, because Jack and Warren had always come home from school together, they were a tight team and did not often seek out the company of other boys. But with Warren away training to be an officer at Sandhurst, Jack was now alone. When he learned that Arthur was at home sick, he went next door to visit him. To his surprise Jack noticed a copy of *Myths of the Norsemen* on the nightstand beside Arthur's bed. Jack pointed to it. "Do *you* like that?" he asked.

"Do *you* like that?" Arthur replied incredulously.

An hour later the two boys were still discussing myths and legends, and Jack knew he had found a true friend in Arthur.

Meanwhile, the situation in Europe continued to deteriorate. On August 1, Germany declared war on Russia, and two days later France declared war on Germany. Then Germany invaded Belgium in order to march through that country to Paris. In response, Great Britain honored its treaty with France and declared war on Germany on August 4, 1914. And three weeks later, Japan declared war on Germany, honoring its treaty with Great Britain. Not surprisingly, at Sandhurst Warren was fast-tracked in his officers' training so that he would be ready to serve in the war.

In the midst of all this, Jack prepared to go and live with Professor Kirkpatrick, who lived in Great Bookham, Surrey, England. Although Jack was nearing his sixteenth birthday, he was not concerned that he would be conscripted to fight in the war. He was an Irish citizen, not a British citizen, and Britain had no power to call up Irish troops.

Once again Jack caught the boat from Belfast to Liverpool and then on Saturday caught the train to London, where he changed to another train for the final leg of his journey to Bookham. As the train rumbled through the Surrey countryside, the land was not at all how Jack had imagined it to be. The landscape was dotted with hills and wooded valleys, with villages tucked among them. Most of the houses were wooden, with tile roofs, rather than built of brick or stone. When the train finally pulled to a halt at the station at Bookham, William Kirkpatrick was waiting there to meet Jack. Old Knock was a tall, lanky man, standing over six feet tall. He had a bushy moustache and side-whiskers, but his chin was clean-shaven. As Jack shook his hand, he marveled at William Kirkpatrick's clothes. Old Knock was dressed more like a gardener than a professor.

As the two men walked from the station to the Kirkpatrick home, which was called "Gastons," Jack tried to make small talk, commenting on how different the countryside was than he had expected. It was then that Jack learned how exacting Old Knock was.

Instead of responding to Jack's small talk, Old Knock began in his Ulster brogue challenging the premises of what Jack had just said, noting how illogical and pointless his comments were. Jack knew right then that he was going to have to think a little harder before talking to the professor.

Over tea at Gastons, Old Knock outlined his study regimen for Jack. "On Monday we will begin by reading Homer in Greek."

Jack gulped. He did not know Greek, so how was he supposed to read a book in a language he did not know? His objection did not seem to faze Old Knock, and on Monday morning the professor walked into the small upstairs study that was Jack's classroom. He opened a copy of the *Iliad* to Book I and read the first two pages aloud in Greek. Jack could not understand a word of it. Old Knock then translated the first hundred lines of the book into English and handed the page, along with a Greek lexicon, over to Jack. He told Jack to study what he had done and begin trying his hand at translating some more lines himself.

Jack did what he was told, studying Homer's Greek text, Old Knock's translation, and the lexicon. Slowly over the next several weeks, he began to grasp the basics of Greek. Before Jack was aware of it, he was not just translating the words into English in his head but was thinking and understanding in Greek as he read.

Albert Lewis had been concerned that Jack would find living with Professor and Mrs. Kirkpatrick lonely and boring, but nothing could have been further from the truth. Jack loved being the only boy in the house, and he and the professor soon worked out a routine that was agreeable to both of them.

Every morning at eight o'clock, the smell of sizzling bacon and tomatoes filled the house, and Jack enjoyed a hearty breakfast, complete with Irish soda bread. It reminded him of home and put him in a good mood for the rest of the day. Then it was upstairs to study and translate from nine till eleven, when Mrs. Kirkpatrick brought Jack a cup of tea. Jack then continued his schoolwork until lunchtime. After lunch he took a long walk through the countryside and settled back down to work again at about five o'clock in the afternoon. At seven o'clock he shared the evening meal with his hosts and then read happily until bedtime.

One thing Jack did not have to do for the first time in his life was attend church on Sundays. Professor Kirkpatrick was a self-avowed atheist who continually challenged Jack to prove the little he still believed about God. This was an exacting task, and Jack soon gave up trying, admitting to himself and Old Knock that he had doubts about Christianity in particular and religious faith in general. This led to many long conversations about why the professor believed that the Bible was not true and that God did not exist.

Jack had been at Great Bookham only about a month when he received a letter from Warren telling him that he had been commissioned as a second lieutenant in the Royal ASC (Army Service Corps), charged with transporting goods and supplies to the soldiers fighting on the frontlines of the war in Europe.

Jack guessed that it would be a matter of only a few weeks before his brother would be on his way to France. He was right. In November Albert sent word that Jack was to come back to Belfast to say goodbye to Warren. It was a short and awkward visit. Every time Jack went home, he could think of less to say to his father than the visit before, and Warren was now strangely grown up, dressed in his tailored serge uniform with shiny brass buttons.

On his return to Great Bookham, Jack felt more isolated than ever, and he threw himself into study. He soaked up information like a sponge, continuing on in his Greek studies and adding Latin, French, and Italian to the mix. He also discovered new authors and new books. His new favorite book was George MacDonald's *Phantastes.* This book revolved around a dream in which a hero named Anodos wakes up in a strange world. A stranger, who later turns out to be his dead grandmother, guides him through a hole in a writing desk to the land of the fairies. Everything about the book intrigued Jack; the book built on so many of the stories he had heard since he was a young child. Jack also realized that he loved the sound of the English language, and he set his sights on becoming a poet.

Under Professor Kirkpatrick's tutelage Jack found that any vestige of his Christian faith was completely eroded. Sometimes Jack put his thoughts on paper in letters to his new friend Arthur Greeves. In one letter he wrote that he thought Christianity was built on myths and that Jesus had been seen as a god only after he died. He also admitted that he was quite relieved to live without believing in a "bogey who is going to torture me forever" if he failed to do everything that the Bible mandated. Any God that would do that, he argued, was "a spirit more cruel and barbarous than any man." Jack wanted to make it absolutely clear to Arthur that he had outgrown the Christian religion.

Two years rolled by, and in November 1916, Jack celebrated his eighteenth birthday. By now he had turned into a solid, stocky young man whose high-school education was almost behind him and who now had to make a choice about his future. Jack knew that if he went home to Ireland he could avoid the war, since the British government did not conscript on Irish soil. But if he stayed in England and applied to study at Oxford, as he desired to do, he would eventually be called up to serve in the army and sent to fight in the deadly trenches of France. Jack wrestled with his conscience over what to do and eventually made his peace, applying to Oxford and waiting for the call to arms.

Having made his decision, Jack refused to spend another minute thinking about the war. He wrote, "I put the war on one side to a degree which some people will think shameful and some incredible. Others will call it a flight from reality. I maintain that it was rather a treaty with reality, a fixing of a frontier. I said to my country, in effect, 'You shall have me on a certain date, not before. I will die in your wars if need be, but till then I shall live my own life.'"

As it turned out, getting accepted to University College in Oxford proved more difficult than Jack had expected. Jack excelled in English and languages, but he hated science and mathematics and had spent little time studying them. But to become a member of the university he had to pass an examination that included his two worst subjects.

Jack took one last semester at Great Bookham with Professor Kirkpatrick to brush up on science and mathematics, but his heart was not in it. Whenever he was left unsupervised, he turned to studying German and Italian. It was a weak effort, and it resulted in Jack's failing the entrance exams for the college.

Fortunately for him, the master of University College took pity on Jack because his other grades were so high. He allowed Jack to begin studying at the college, with the promise that he would work hard and pass his failed entrance tests in science and mathematics before he graduated.

On April 28, 1917, C. S. Lewis began his studies at Oxford. But as he entered the hallowed gates of Oxford as a scholar, the threat of fighting in the war loomed over his head.

Chapter 5

Into the Trenches

As Jack strolled around University College, Oxford, on the first day of the term, he wondered whether he had entered a university or a hospital. Actually, it was a bit of both. Half of the college had been converted into wards to accommodate soldiers wounded while fighting in the trenches of France. The other half of the school still functioned as a college, but it had only twelve students in attendance, including Jack. The rest of the student body had gone off to fight in the war. Encountering bandaged, wheelchair-bound men in the Radcliffe Quadrangle was a solemn reminder to Jack that it was only a matter of weeks before he would be transitioning from student to soldier and that he might possibly return to Oxford wounded—or worse, as an invalid.

Jack's professors refused to give him any assignments, since they knew he would not be there for long, so Jack found himself in the strange position of being at college with no work to do. He whiled away the hours reading in the college's wood-paneled library and wandering the grounds of the university. The architecture, some of which dated back to the college's founding in 1249, fascinated Jack, and he often sketched his impressions of what he saw.

The town of Oxford itself also delighted Jack. It was spring, and Jack reveled in the blossoms that festooned the trees and the colorful flowers bursting forth everywhere. He also liked how quiet the town was. There were few cars in the place. Horses and carriages were still the main form of transport, while students scurried about decked out in their academic robes. All in all, Jack thought it was the perfect environment for study.

As he studied, Jack knew that his easy life at college could not last, not with Europe embroiled in such a major war. And sure enough, in May he was called up to go and fight for Mother England. The transition was surprisingly easy for Jack to make, since he was assigned to the Cadet Battalion, which was housed at Keble College, Oxford, located a short distance from University College. Once at Keble, the young draftees were assigned to barracks by alphabetical order. Jack found himself bunking next to Edward Courtnay Francis Moore, who insisted on being called simply "Paddy." Paddy and Jack hit it off from the beginning; both had roots in Ireland, and both could have avoided being drafted but chose to fight out of a sense of duty and honor.

Basic training itself was mild. Nothing, Jack joked, compared to the harsh realities of attending an English boarding school. The battalion marched around the countryside and often slept in the open air, an activity that Jack had always loved.

Paddy's mother, Janie Moore, who had separated from her husband years before, came to stay in Oxford to be close to her only son. Paddy's twelve-year-old sister Maureen came along as well. Jack was soon drawn into their congenial family atmosphere and before long found himself spending all his days off with the Moores.

When the four-week period of basic training was over, Jack was commissioned as a second lieutenant in the Somerset Light Infantry and was to report to a camp near Plymouth to take charge of a group of new trainees, while Paddy was to be sent straight to France. Each of them, however, was given a month's leave before having to report to his new posting. For the first two weeks of his leave, Jack went to Bristol and stayed with Paddy's family before returning to Belfast to visit his father.

Before Jack and Paddy parted, they made a solemn vow to each other. Jack promised that if Paddy were to be killed in the fighting, he would make sure that his mother and younger sister were looked after, and Paddy promised to be a "son" to Albert Lewis if Jack should be killed. The promises were a relief to both young men, although, of course, they hoped that neither of them would ever have to fulfill them.

When Jack finally arrived at his new posting in Plymouth, he learned that his new job was remarkably simple. All he had to do was march a group of new recruits in training out of their barracks in the morning and deliver them to their instructors and then march them back to barracks again at night. By then the men were so exhausted that they got up to little mischief.

After a month at Plymouth, Jack received orders to report to South Hampton for transport to France. It was now time for him to face the grim reality of life on the battlefield. Jack was granted forty-eight hours' leave before he had to report to South Hampton for transport, so he headed straight for Bristol to stay with Janie and Maureen Moore. He also telegraphed his father, hoping that he would make a quick trip across the Irish Sea to say goodbye to his son.

Unexplainably, Albert refused to make the trip to Bristol. At the same time, Janie Moore fussed over Jack, making sure that he had a good last two days in England. The contrast between his father's and Janie's reactions had a profound impact on Jack, who soon came to regard Janie, Maureen, and Paddy as his real family—apart from Warren. Jack felt these were the people who cared about him most in the world.

After two wonderful days in Bristol, Jack found himself on a ship bound for France. He spent his first night in France in a huge tent, sleeping on a plank bed alongside a hundred fellow officers. Twelve days later, on his nineteenth birthday, November 29, 1917, Jack arrived at the battlefront in the trenches of France's Somme Valley. Here for the first time he could see the German army, the common enemy of the Allied forces.

The soldiers in the battalion Jack was assigned to were a mixture of West Country farmers; professional men such as lawyers, accountants, and teachers; and university students like himself. Jack enjoyed the conversations he had with many of the men and noted the strange camaraderie that war produced among such a diverse group of people. He also enjoyed reading the literary books that the men swapped among themselves. Often the books were so worn from constantly being read that they were held together by pieces of string. None of the men seemed to mind what condition the books were in so long as they had something to read to take their minds off the deplorable conditions around them.

Jack found himself living in a muddy trench in a landscape that had been completely denuded of trees and any other vegetation by three years of constant shelling by each side. In front of the trench was a quagmire, a strip of land laced with razor wire and decaying bodies. On the other side of this strip of land, which was called "no-man's-land," were the German trenches. A constant barrage of artillery fire raged back and forth between the two sides, and the trenches were so close that you had to be careful not to inadvertently put your head up. The price for doing so was usually a bullet in the head from a German sharpshooter.

Jack watched as countless lives on both sides were lost trying to capture and hold some portion of no-man's-land. Each time Jack led his men over the top of the trench to fight for a small piece of this forsaken strip of land, he never knew whether he would return. Bullets and artillery shells laced with shrapnel would rain down on them, killing and mutilating soldiers. Some of the mud holes in no-man's-land were so deep that it was not uncommon during the fighting for a soldier to become trapped in mud up to his waist or chest.

Fortunately for Jack, each time he went over the top, he managed to return. The smell of rotting bodies filled the air as the men huddled together to eat what each man knew could well be his last meal. In this environment Jack tried to take his mind off things by not only reading books but also writing poems in a small notebook.

In late November, Jack learned that Warren had been made a captain, and soon after that Warren was training at a Mechanical Transport School in France. The Lewis brothers were both in France, and both were in mortal danger.

Despite the grimness of the trenches, humorous moments sometimes presented themselves. One such moment occurred when Jack and his men were on patrol away from the trenches. The men came upon a seemingly deserted and bombed-out farmhouse. Jack grew suspicious of the place and stopped to confer with Sergeant Ayers, upon whose judgment in military matters Jack, as a junior officer, had come to depend. The two men decided to proceed cautiously, with Jack and the rest of the men waiting in hiding while Sergeant Ayers took several men with him and moved in on the farmhouse from the back.

Jack heard the sergeant and his men crash through the back door of the farmhouse. Thirty young German soldiers immediately came tumbling out the front door of the house in a panic. The Germans, obviously terrified, threw down their rifles when they saw Jack. Cautiously Jack walked over to them while the rest of his men came out of hiding with their rifles at the ready. As he got closer to the soldiers, Jack could clearly see the terror in their eyes. He tried to talk to them in German, but in the excitement of the moment, all that came was stammer instead of German words. So Jack switched to French. At hearing his words in French, the German soldiers fell to their knees in surrender and begged him for mercy.

After a few minutes Jack was able to work out what was going on. It appeared that the rumor among the Germans was that French soldiers were taking no prisoners, choosing instead to kill their captives on the battlefield. When the Germans heard Jack's French, they had feared the worst. Jack could see the relief in their eyes when they learned that he was English.

As the captured soldiers were marched away, Jack felt proud of himself. Sergeant Ayers then stepped forward and pointed out to Jack that in such situations in the future, it would be better if Jack drew his weapon!

Not long after capturing the German soldiers, Jack became one of the lucky ones, if anyone is lucky in war. He came down with a case of trench fever, a flulike illness spread by ticks, and had to spend three weeks in the hospital at Le Tréport. His time in the hospital was an island of calm in a seemingly endless sea of destruction. Jack spent hours reading books by G. K. Chesterton from the hospital library and writing letters to his friends and family. When he recovered from his illness, Jack returned to the frontlines refreshed and began writing more poems for his collection, which he had titled *Spirits of Bondage*.

By midwinter, Jack was astonished to realize that he had survived five months in the trenches, and he began to wonder how much longer his luck would last. On April 15, 1918, he thought the day that his luck ran out had arrived. Jack was in the trenches at Mount Bernenchon, near Lillers, France, as the Battle of Arras got under way. Jack was ordered to take his men "over the top" and attack the German line. The plan called for Allied artillery to pound the Germans with heavy shells. As Jack's platoon moved forward, the artillery fire was to advance ahead of them, softening up the Germans' lines.

Jack ordered his men to attach their bayonets to the end of their rifles in preparation for the battle. As they did so, the Allied artillery fire began right on schedule. Heavy, explosive shells impregnated with shrapnel to inflict maximum damage on the Germans began to stream above the trenches. Jack waited for several minutes for the shells to do their work, and then he gave the order. "Over the top, men," he barked.

Jack, along with the rest of his platoon, clambered up one of the rickety wooden ladders that led out of the muddy trench. Once over the top, the men began advancing toward the German trenches. Sure enough, the artillery fire was doing its job, silencing most of the German machine guns.

Everything was going according to plan until Jack noticed that instead of staying ahead of them, the Allied artillery fire was getting dangerously close to the advancing men. And then to everyone's horror, the shells began falling among the advancing British soldiers. All around soldiers were being blown to bits or torn apart by shrapnel from shells fired by their own side. As Jack looked frantically over at Sergeant Ayers, who was advancing beside him, he heard an ear-shattering boom and saw a bright flash, and then Jack's world went blank and silent. Jack fell face first into the dirt.

Chapter 6

An Oxford Scholar

Jack regained consciousness, aware that his mouth was filled with dirt but lacking the energy to spit it out. Slowly he lifted his head and looked around. He was still on the battlefield, only now it felt to him like it was all a dream, like seeing something through foggy glasses. A bloodied, lifeless body, minus its legs, lay beside him. Jack wondered for a moment whether he still had his legs. He got his answer when he tried to get up. Although he did not have the strength to stand up, he did manage to make it onto all fours—he still had his legs and arms!

Jack began to crawl away from the sounds of screaming and moaning, away from the carnage, struggling over the mangled body parts of fellow soldiers and through muddy bomb craters. With each movement he could feel searing pain pulse through his body, as though a lightning bolt had hit him.

Jack had no idea how far he had crawled before he heard a shout. "Hey, lads, there's a live one here." Then a voice closer to him said, "Lie down, sonny, and we'll roll you onto this stretcher."

Relief surged through Jack's body as he surrendered himself to the care of the stretcher bearers. Jack had done all he could to keep himself alive. Now his fate was in the hands of others.

Two days passed before Jack was conscious enough to comprehend what had happened to him. The story was basic—nothing heroic—unless taking "friendly fire" in a hellhole was heroic in its own right. Jack had been hit by shrapnel in three places: the back of his left hand, his chest, and his left thigh. Fortunately the shards of shrapnel had not lodged in any vital organs, and the doctors were confident that Jack would eventually make a full recovery. Going back into battle immediately was out of the question, however, and Jack began a long journey back to full health.

As he lay in a hospital bed in Étaples, France, Jack learned that Sergeant Ayers had died in the same blast that had injured him. And there was more bad news. Paddy Moore was missing in action. Jack propped himself up in bed and wrote to his father, explaining the new developments:

> 14 May 1918
>
> I am doing exceedingly well, and can now lie on my right side (not of course on my left)

> which is a great treat after you have been on your back for a few weeks. . . . The wound under my arm is worse than a flesh wound, as the bit of metal which went in there is not in my chest . . . this however is nothing to worry about, as it is doing no harm. . . . I am told that I can carry it about for the rest of my life without any evil results. . . .
>
> My friend Mrs. Moore is in great trouble—Paddy has been missing for over a month, and is almost certainly dead. Of all my own particular set at Keble he has been the first to go, and it is pathetic to remember that he at least was always certain that he would come through.

Ten days after writing the letter, Jack was transferred from France to Endsleigh Palace Hospital in London. From there he wrote to his father once again, this time begging him to come and visit him in the hospital. But Albert stubbornly refused to break his daily routine to make the trip to England. It was a bitter blow to Jack, especially when he contrasted it with the loving attention Janie Moore was lavishing upon him. Paddy was still missing in action, and instead of feeling sorry for herself, Mrs. Moore spent her energy helping Jack get well.

During his stay in the hospital, Jack came to realize that his wounds were not only physical but also psychological. Every night he dreamed of death, of being buried alive in a trench or shot to pieces with shrapnel. Each dream became more vivid as he learned that more of his friends had been killed in the fighting. In September news came that Paddy Moore was in fact dead. Of the six friends Jack had made at Keble during basic training, he was now the only one still alive.

Jack continued his slow convalescence and was transferred to a hospital in Bristol, where he was close to the Moores. He now had a new and permanent responsibility—taking care of Mrs. Moore and Maureen. It was a task he took very seriously, and in many ways he viewed his obligations to them as more important than those to his own family.

While recuperating in the hospital, Jack edited the poems he had written in the trenches on the frontlines of battle, and he added other poems to the collection. When he was finished, he submitted the collection to a publisher in London. Word soon arrived back that the poems—*Spirits of Bondage*—were to be published in book form. Jack was about to become a published author. It was a thrilling time for him, and it blunted the agonies of war for a moment.

By November 11, 1918, Jack was almost well enough to be sent back to France to fight, but to everyone's relief and delight, on that day Germany surrendered. The Great War in Europe was over. Jack and Warren had both survived the fighting. Now Jack could make plans for his life. His first priority was to visit his father at Little Lea in Belfast.

Jack arrived in Belfast two days after Christmas in 1918 for a bittersweet reunion with his father. Warren was already there, having arrived several days before, and the two brothers and their father toasted the end of four grueling years of war and the fact that both brothers had survived the gruesome battlefields of France.

Warren, as a career army officer, was on leave and due to return shortly to France and then go to Belgium to help bring civil order to those war-torn places. Jack was eager to return to University College in Oxford and begin his studies in earnest. And on this front there was some good news. With so many young British men dead as a result of the war, University College, along with the other colleges at Oxford, was half empty. A university could not run without students, and so the university board had decided to make it easier for students to enter the institution. They rewrote the rules so that soldiers returning from war did not have to pass the entrance exams, thus freeing Jack from the burden of having to pass the mathematics and sciences parts of the exams—something he had already failed twice.

This was a huge relief to Jack, because he doubted that he would ever have been able to pass the tests. Such failure would have led to his eventually being thrown out of University College. The war, for all its ugliness, had bestowed on Jack one great gift—the opportunity to become an Oxford scholar.

Oxford had always been a beautiful place, but in January 1919, when Jack returned to begin attending class at University College, the contrast to the muddy trenches of France was overwhelming. Jack quickly settled in to his new schedule, rising before daybreak to watch the winter sun creep over the horizon and ignite the ancient towers of the town in a golden glow.

The close relationship Jack had forged with the Moores continued to deepen, and soon Janie Moore and her daughter moved into a rented house in Oxford so that they could all be a "family." Jack realized it was an odd arrangement, and he tried to shield his father from the details. This was difficult, however, because he had made a financial commitment to help Mrs. Moore and Maureen, a commitment he could not fulfill without a generous allowance from his father. On top of this, Janie Moore constantly changed houses and expected Jack to fix up each new house to her liking. In between his studies Jack laid carpet, painted walls, and dug gardens. Remarkably, he was able to keep up his grades.

During his first year at University College, Jack was required to live on campus. But in his second year he moved into the Moore home and became a permanent member of the household. Again he avoided explaining the situation to his father and had all of his mail directed to him through the college.

Despite all the external changes, Jack matured as a reader and writer, a fact reflected in the honors he began piling up. In April 1920 he won a first-class degree in classical studies, the Chancellor's English Essay Prize, followed by another first-class degree in literature in 1923.

One incident, though, cast a shadow over this time. In March 1921 Jack learned of the death of his old professor, William Kirkpatrick, "Old Knock." Jack wrote down his thoughts upon hearing the news. "Poor old Kirk, I owe him in the intellectual sphere as much as one human being can owe another. That he enabled me to win a scholarship is the least he did for me. It was an atmosphere of unrelenting clearness and rigid honesty of thought that one breathed from living with him."

By this time Jack was sure he wanted to follow in Old Knock's footsteps and become an English tutor. He applied for every job that became available at the university. He was passed over for the first two positions, but he won a job on his third attempt. The position was that of a substitute for a philosophy tutor who was on leave in the United States for a year. Jack thrived in his new position and greatly appreciated finally earning his own money. He felt he no longer had to be dishonest about where his father's money was being spent. The job also furnished Jack with his first experience at public speaking, and in a letter to his father Jack outlined how he was approaching his forthcoming lectures: "I am to lecture twice a week next term, which comes to fourteen hours talking in all. . . . I rather fancy I could tell the world everything I know about everything in five hours—and Lord, you hear curates grumbling because they have to preach for about twenty minutes a week. . . . [I] must learn that slow deliberated method dear to the true lecturer."

Jack soon adjusted to lecturing and began to enjoy the challenge of engaging his students in the subject. He decided not to read straight from lecture notes, because doing so, more often than not, put his students to sleep. Instead, he practiced using sparse notes scribbled on slips of paper and expanding them to fit the allotted time of the lecture. He also enjoyed being part of two worlds—the heady, intellectual world of the Oxford tutor and the down-to-earth role of a family man at the Moores. His days fell into a pattern. He had breakfast served in his college rooms each weekday, followed by tutorials for the rest of the morning, before walking to the Moore house for lunch. Following lunch he did a few odd jobs that Janie Moore invariably had lined up for him to do, and then he walked the long route back to college, where he either lectured or tutored for the afternoon. His day usually ended with formal dinner in the University College Hall, after which the faculty often retired to a common room to continue with any lively conversation that had been started over dinner. On Friday nights, Jack would retire to the Moore house, where he would stay until Sunday afternoon.

Jack found that this new lifestyle suited him immensely, and so at the end of the year he applied for a fellowship in the English department at Magdalen College, Oxford. Much to his delight, he won the position and moved into his rooms there. The rooms were located in what was called "New Building," despite the fact that it was built in 1793 as the medieval college outgrew itself. Jack's only disappointment was learning that he had to furnish his college rooms himself. This included finding tables, chairs, curtains, rugs, fire irons, a coal box, a bed, and bookshelves. Several friends came to the rescue and loaned him bits and pieces, and his father sent him a check to cover the cost of the rest of the furnishings.

Over the summer, Jack, Janie, and Maureen celebrated Jack's new position, and the financial relief it brought to them all, with a trip to Somerset.

Magdalen College was located just outside the old city wall of Oxford beside the Cherwell River. Although most of the college was constructed during the fifteenth century, it did not have the closed-in feel of many of the other medieval colleges of the town. The ancient buildings were clustered around lawns and gardens, and a deer park bordered the college to the north, where the deer sheltered themselves under clusters of old elm trees. Across the river was a meadow, where wildflowers bloomed in the spring. Around the meadow ran Addison's Walk, which also passed the secluded Fellows' Garden. Jack loved the location. His large sitting room in New Building faced north and looked out across the deer park, while the view from his small sitting room and bedroom looked south across a broad lawn to the main buildings of Magdalen College.

Jack embraced his new "home college" with great enthusiasm and soon established his routine. He arrived for breakfast at eight in the dining room with the college's other fellows, among them Paul Victor Mendelssohn Benecke. Paul was the grandson of composer Felix Mendelssohn, and senior fellow at the college. He was a deeply spiritual man whom

Jack loved to talk with in the mornings. Paul's character and spirit had a deep impact on Jack.

Jack also enjoyed the company of J. A. Smith, the Wayneflete professor of moral and metaphysical philosophy. J. A., as everyone called him, was a Scotsman who always seemed to come to breakfast pondering some piece of information or concept that Jack found fascinating. J. A. was also a stickler for using the correct meaning of words, a practice that he passed on to Jack.

Adam Fox, dean of the divinity school, was another colleague Jack enjoyed having breakfast with. He had a gentle and devout manner about him that intrigued and challenged Jack.

Following breakfast Jack returned to his rooms and prepared himself for his first tutorial, which started at nine. For the tutorial, a student would come to Jack's rooms on the hour. The student would sit in an armchair by the fire while Jack sat opposite on a couch reviewing the student's essay and asking him to explain and expand on the meanings of things he had written.

In the evenings Jack would eat dinner with the other fellows and students of the college in the hall, after which, as the tutors and fellows at University College had done, they all retired to the senior common room to continue their conversations started over dinner.

At the same time as Jack won the fellowship at Magdalen College, his immediate obligations to the Moores began to lessen when Maureen left for college to train as a music teacher. Yet Jack still found that his emotional attachment to Janie Moore, now fifty-three years old, was as strong as ever, and he longed to set up a permanent home for the two of them to live in.

Jack's ability to finally do this was made possible, indirectly, through Albert Lewis. Jack's father had become seriously ill, and in August 1929 Jack returned to Little Lea to visit him. He spent close to a month at home in Belfast, running errands for his father and bathing, shaving, and cooking for him. During this time Albert underwent an operation, wherein the doctor discovered that he had cancer. The doctor supposed that Albert would live at least another year or more. Jack made arrangements for his father's convalescence and returned to Oxford on September 22. He expected to have several more visits with his father.

Chapter 7

Leaving Ireland Behind

Two days after his return to Oxford from Belfast, a telegram arrived for Jack from his father's doctor. Albert Lewis's health was failing fast, and he was not expected to live long. Jack threw a few belongings into a suitcase and headed for the train station to start the journey back to Ireland. Unfortunately, Albert died before Jack reached Belfast. He was sixty-six years old.

His father's death was a cruel blow for Jack, who was left feeling alone and remorseful that he had not been kinder and more respectful to his father during his adolescence. Since the death of his mother, Jack had never been able to feel close to his father, though he was grateful for the monthly allowance Albert had always sent him. In his grief Jack wished

Warren were there with him at Little Lea instead of being stationed thousands of miles away in Shanghai, China. Jack wrote to his older brother, telling him of the funeral and trying to keep him informed as to the decisions that needed to be made regarding their inheritance. On a more personal note, Jack also wrote about the emotional impact their father's death was having on him:

> As time goes on, the thing that emerges is that, whatever else he was, he was a terrific *personality.* You remember "Johnson is dead. Let us go to the next. There is none. No man can be said to put you in the mind of Johnson." How he filled the room. How hard it was to realize that physically he was not a big man. Our whole world is either direct or indirect testimony to the same fact. . . . The way we enjoyed going to Little Lea, and the way we hated it, and the way we enjoyed hating it; as you say, one can't grasp that *that* is over.

Both Jack and Warren realized that it made no sense to keep Little Lea. Jack's only reason for visiting the place in the past few years had been because his father lived there, and Warren was now posted overseas most of the time. Yet both brothers had to admit that they were attached to the house where they had spent the happiest part of their childhood. It was painful to think of selling it and of another family moving into the house and changing things around. It was so painful, in fact, that Warren came up with all kinds of ideas to reconstruct their "Little End Room" in the attic in Jack's rooms at Oxford. Warren was constantly writing and asking Jack about the fate of their boyhood toys. After several rounds of pleading letters from his brother, Jack decided it would be unwise to move much out of Little Lea until Warren was there to add his input. He had the house boarded up for the remainder of the winter and returned to Oxford.

Back at Oxford, Jack threw himself into his work, though many things were developing within and around him that would change the course of his life. The first was his growing friendship with another Oxford professor, John Ronald Reuel Tolkien. J. R. R. Tolkien—or Tollers, as he was known—was the Rawlingson professor of Anglo-Saxon and fellow of Pembroke College, Oxford, and he and Jack had met in 1926 at a combined meeting of the English faculty at Oxford. The two men soon discovered that they had a mutual love of myth and medieval poetry, and before long Tolkien invited Jack to join a group called the Kolbitar, or Coalbiters, a Norse name for a group that sat around the fire talking. However, the Coalbiters did a lot more than just talk. Tolkien set about teaching the members of the group the Norse language. Jack was delighted to find that Tollers used the same method for learning a language that Professor Kirkpatrick (Old Knock) had used with him, and his experience learning German and Anglo-Saxon made the undertaking relatively easy.

The friendship between the two men continued to grow. Tolkien came from a Catholic background, and although Jack did not consider himself a religious man, he soon realized that he had grown up with a strong prejudice against Catholics. At first he found this prejudice hard to break, but the more time he spent with Tolkien, the more he liked him as a person and admired his intellect. As Jack himself had done as a boy back in Belfast, Tolkien had created in his head a vast mythical kingdom peopled with all manner of creatures often engaged in epic battles with each other. Tolkien referred to his mythical world as "Middle-earth." But whereas Jack had left his boyhood make-believe world behind, Tolkien had continued to develop his and was now beginning to write down the stories of "Middle-earth." And the stories were good, as Jack found out when Tollers asked him to read the manuscript he was presently working on. The manuscript was titled *Lay of Leithian,* and Tolkien had been working on it for several years. While the story was not yet finished, Jack was enthralled with it, especially the way Tolkien so deftly wove ancient myths and sagas into his work. Jack was so impressed that he wrote a note to Tolkien:

> I sat up late last night and read the *Geste* [adventure or tale] as far as to where Beren and his gnomish allies defeat the patrol of orcs above the sources of the Narog and disguise themselves in the *reaf* [an Old English word

> meaning "garments, weapons taken from the slain"]. I can quite honestly say that it is ages since I have had an evening of such delight; and that personal interest in a friend's work had very little to do with it. I should have enjoyed it just as well if I'd picked it up in a bookshop, by an unknown author. The two things that come out clearly are the sense of reality in the background and the mythical value.

Jack wished that he could write with the same caliber and voice as Tolkien. But the truth was that while Jack liked to write, he was having a hard time focusing in on what to write about.

Tolkien and Jack had many discussions about Tolkien's writing. At the same time Jack was reading G. K. Chesterton's book *The Everlasting Man.* The combination of the message of Chesterton's book and Tolkien's devout faith began to have an impact on Jack, who found a certain compelling logic in *The Everlasting Man* that caused him to reevaluate how he thought about God. Eventually Jack decided that he did believe in a God—not a biblical God, but a supreme being of some type who tried to communicate with mankind. Once Jack came to this conclusion, he started to attend the Anglican church as a statement to himself and others that he no longer considered himself to be an atheist.

In late April 1930, seven months after Albert Lewis's death, Warren finally arrived back in Ireland after a long and eventful voyage from China via the United States. The Lewis brothers reunited at Little Lea and set about the momentous task of breaking up the family home. They divided everything in the house into three piles: one for things they could not part with, another for things they wanted to give away, and the third for things they wanted to sell. Room by room they made their way through Little Lea, emptying each room, until finally they came to their attic hideaway. Here they came upon the large trunk that held their toys, most of which had figured as characters in Jack's fantasy Animal-Land and Warren's India. In the end the two brothers decided not to open the trunk but instead carried it to the vegetable garden, where they dug a hole and buried it.

Once everything in the house had been disposed of, Jack and Warren visited their parents' graves, the dirt on Albert's grave still freshly turned.

During their time together, Warren confessed to Jack that he was under pressure to resign from the army because he had a problem with alcohol. This did not surprise Jack, who realized that both his older brother and his father had melancholy personalities and did not cope very well with unpleasant or sad situations, and both of them used alcohol freely and frequently to help get them through such times.

Jack and Warren were also faced with another problem. Their father's estate had turned out to be not worth as much as either brother had thought. Little Lea could be sold for twenty-three hundred pounds, but when this amount was split, it was not enough for either of them to buy a house. It became clear that Jack and Warren would have to pool their money if they wanted to replace their childhood home with a similar place in Oxford.

In fact, the real problem was not so much that the brothers needed to pool their money to buy a home together but that Jack could not imagine separating from his "other family." Any house he and Warren bought would have to be big enough to share with Mrs. Moore and Maureen. Though Jack harbored secret doubts about all four of them getting along for the rest of their lives, he felt they had to try.

Back in Oxford, Jack, Warren, and Janie set about the task of finding a suitable house to buy. Jack wanted the house to be as much like Little Lea as possible, surrounded by open fields and close to picturesque walks. Of course this was quite a tall order to fulfill, especially on their budget, but eventually Jack and Janie stumbled upon a property called The Kilns. It was called this because of two large kilns that stood like upturned flowerpots beside the house. These kilns had once been used for baking bricks for buildings in the Oxford area. The Kilns was located just outside Oxford and sat on nine acres of wooded land that also contained a lake. On the far side of the two kilns stood a large, open shed that had been used for drying the bricks. Jack and Janie viewed the house on July 7, 1930, and they immediately fell in love with it, especially the grounds.

Several days later Warren returned to Oxford on leave and went to see The Kilns. He, too, was taken with how beautiful the grounds were, but he thought the house might be a little too small for four adults to live in. Nonetheless, he could not deny the beauty of the setting and Jack and Janie's excitement at the thought of living there. The three of them made an offer to buy the place for thirty-three hundred pounds. On July 16 they received word that their offer had been accepted, and arrangements were then made for a mortgage to cover the portion of the price they did not have. Jack and Warren also signed over their interest in the place so that the house belonged exclusively to Janie Moore and would be passed on to her daughter Maureen when Janie died.

On October 10, 1930, Warren returned to Oxford on leave and helped Jack, Maureen, and Janie move from a rented house in Hillsboron into their new home, The Kilns.

As Jack pushed open the front door of The Kilns and moved in, he wondered what this new phase of his life would be like.

Chapter 8

A Failure of Imagination

The year 1931 began with a long walk, a four-day, fifty-four-mile walk, in fact. Before Warren's leave was over and he returned to Bulford in Southern England to resume his post as assistant to the officer in charge of supplies and transport, he and Jack decided to take a walking tour of the Wye Valley, located on the Welsh border. The tour was a great success. Each day Warren and Jack walked about twelve miles, taking plenty of time to stop along the way and study the birds and animals that crossed their path. Each night they stopped at a local pub, where they ate a hearty meal before going to sleep in a guesthouse. The experience reminded the Lewis brothers of the cycling trips they had made as boys in Ireland, and both men pledged to go on another walking tour when Warren had more leave. The following week Warren headed back to Bulford.

The following term was a busy one for Jack, though he determined to go to church each Sunday as an outward sign that he now believed in some kind of higher being, which he was content to call "God." Still, Jack had nagging doubts about his loosely defined set of beliefs and secretly wondered whether there was more to it. He knew that he had embarked on a journey, but he was nervous and unsure as to where that journey might lead.

Some of his doubts surfaced later that year when, on September 19, Jack invited Tolkien and his friend Hugo Dyson to Magdalen College for dinner. Dyson had been an undergraduate with Tolkien at Exeter College and was now a lecturer at Reading University. He also had been a friend of Lawrence of Arabia and knew Virginia Woolf, Bertrand Russell, and D. H. Lawrence. The conversation over dinner was lively and far ranging.

Following dinner the three men set out for a stroll on Addison's Walk, the one-mile circuit that wound its way beneath stands of beech trees. As they walked, the discussion turned to the nature of myth and religion. Tolkien made the point that myths and legends originated in God and that they carry some aspect of truth about God. In fact, in writing stories based around these myths, a writer may actually be doing God's work. Jack nodded in agreement. Tolkien then explained that the Christian story was itself a myth created by a real God, whose dying could transform the lives of those who believed in him. But Jack found this point harder to agree with. He pointed out that he could not see how the death of "someone else" two thousand years before could help much in the here and now, except perhaps so far as that person's example might help us.

Tolkien walked on a few paces in silence, Jack on one side of him and Dyson on the other. When he finally spoke, he pointed out to Jack that his failure to grasp the central core of the Christian message was mostly a failure of imagination on Jack's part. He pointed out that Jack had no difficulty in grasping and drawing meaning from the ancient myths of the Greeks and the Norse, but when it came to Christianity, he wanted to put on the cap of a rationalist and wrestle with the logic of the story rather than accept it and draw truth and meaning from it.

At that point a gust of wind rustled the branches of the trees above them, and the sound reminded Jack of a passage from his friend Owen Barfield's book *Poetic Diction*. Barfield had made the point that in ancient times people did not make a distinction between myth and fact, between the metaphorical and the literal meaning of words. He pointed out that the word *spirit*, or *spiritus* in Latin, meant breath. Today's rationalist may choose to distinguish between the mere breath and some other elevated state, but those who first formed the language made no such distinction. When they experienced the wind blowing, it was not *like* someone breathing; rather, it was the actual breath of God.

Tollers looked up at the rustling trees and the flickering stars beyond. As if reading Jack's mind, he noted that while we speak of stars and trees as material entities, those who first formed the words thought of them very differently. To them the stars were living silver that burst into flame in answer to the music in the mind of God. All creation, Tollers said, reiterating his earlier point, is myth-woven. And, he pressed, Jack was missing out on grasping the essential meaning of the Christian story because he would not allow his imagination to embrace it in the same way he embraced the essential truth and meaning of myths. Instead, when he came to Christianity, he was altogether too much the rationalist and empiricist.

It was three o'clock in the morning when Tolkien finally left the group to return home, leaving Jack and Dyson to talk for another hour.

Jack thought a lot about the words Tollers had spoken that night. He found a certain compelling logic in Tolkien's argument. Indeed he did tend to use two different modes of thought when he approached myths and the Christian story, and this was holding him back from discovering the truth of Christianity. He continued to think about the conversation throughout the next week. He still had many questions, but he had to admit that Tolkien's approach made Christianity sound more appealing and believable. Still, Jack wondered whether he could ever fully embrace ideas that seemed odd to him, especially the concept that Jesus was the Son of God and that He died for everyone's sins. It just seemed too fantastic. But then Tolkien's words would come back to him. Was his friend right? Did he, Jack, lack the imagination necessary to believe?

Jack summarized his conversation with Tolkien and Dyson in a letter to his boyhood friend Arthur Greeves:

> Now what Dyson and Tolkien showed me was this: that if I met the idea of sacrifice in a Pagan story I didn't mind it at all: and again, that if I met the idea of god sacrificing himself to himself . . . I liked it very much and was mysteriously moved by it: again, that the idea of the dying and reviving God (Balder, Adonis, Bacchus) similarly moved me provided I met it anywhere *except* in the Gospels. The reason was that in Pagan stories I was prepared to feel the myth as profound and suggestive of meanings beyond my grasp even tho' I could not say in cold prose "what it meant."
>
> Now the story of Christ is simply a true myth: a myth working on us in the same way as the others, but with tremendous difference that *it really happened:* and one must be content to accept it in the same way, remembering that it is God's myth where the others are men's myths: i.e. the Pagan stories are God expressing himself through the minds of

> poets, using such images as He found there, while Christianity is God expressing himself through "real things."

On Monday, September 28, 1931, nine days after his enlightening conversation with Tolkien and Dyson, Jack went on an outing to Whipsnade Zoo with Warren, who was about to leave for China for his second posting there; Janie Moore, her daughter Maureen, and her Irish friend Vera Henry; and their dog, Mr. Papworth. It was decided that the women and Mr. Papworth would ride in the motorcar to the zoo, while Jack would travel with Warren in the side-car of his motorcycle. (It was not an option for Jack to drive. He never held any kind of driver's license, and the idea of controlling a mechanical vehicle seemed to overwhelm him.)

A heavy fog clung to the ground as the group set out. But by the time Jack and Warren reached the city of Thame several miles away, the fog had dissipated and the sun was shining. Along the way the brothers stopped to put gasoline in the motorcycle. By two in the afternoon they reached Whipsnade and stopped on the outskirts of the village to wait for the women. When the car arrived, they all continued in convoy to the zoo.

Jack and Warren particularly enjoyed the zoo, wandering around looking at the animals. Jack made friends with a bear, whom he nicknamed *Bultitude,* and confessed to his brother that his dream was to have a pet bear at The Kilns. (Fortunately for all who lived at The Kilns, he never did manage to get a pet bear. However, Bultitude the bear would appear as a character in the book *That Hideous Strength,* the third book in a space trilogy that Jack would publish in 1945.)

All in all, the trip to Whipsnade Zoo was an uneventful outing, except for one thing. As Jack himself would later put it in his autobiography, *Surprised by Joy,* "I was driven to Whipsnade one sunny morning. When we set out I did not believe that Jesus Christ is the Son of God, and when we reached the zoo I did. Yet I had not exactly spent the journey in thought. Nor in great emotion."

Somewhere between The Kilns and Whipsnade Zoo Jack's imagination had expanded, and he had arrived at the kind of belief that Tolkien had talked to him about. Two days after the trip to the zoo, Jack put his thoughts into words in a letter to Arthur Greeves: "I have just passed on from believing in God to definitely believing in Christ. . . . My long night talk with Dyson and Tolkien had a great deal to do with it."

Jack continued on with his practice of going to the Anglican church in the village of Headington Quarry, near The Kilns. He also began attending the morning chapel service at Magdalen College on weekdays. He felt an obligation to do both, though he did not enjoy the experience much. In fact, he later wrote that he disliked just about everything to do with traditional church services. "To me, religion ought to have been a matter of good men praying alone and meeting by twos and threes to talk of spiritual matters. And then the fussy, time-wasting botheration of it all! The bells, the crowds, the umbrellas, the notices, the bustle, the perpetual arranging and organizing." He even admitted, "Hymns were (and are) extremely disagreeable to me. Of all musical instruments I liked (and like) the organ least. I have, too, a sort of spiritual *gaucherie* [awkwardness] which makes me unapt to participate in any rite."

In January 1932, just three months after his own spiritual renewal, Jack learned that his brother Warren had committed himself to God and had started attending church in Shanghai, where he was once again stationed. This was a great relief to Jack and an encouragement that he was headed in the right direction. Meanwhile, he and Janie planned and supervised the addition of a wing to The Kilns so that Warren would have a place to call his own when he finally left the army and came to live with them for good.

Jack was thirty-three years old when he became a Christian and felt he had a whole new world to explore. As could be expected, he chose to do this exploration via reading and writing. He started writing a novel titled *The Moving Image,* but he soon ran out of motivation and began writing a long poem. He ran out of steam on that project too. It was not until he was back in Belfast visiting his friend Arthur in the spring of 1932 that Jack got a new idea for a book, which he would call *The Pilgrim's Regress.* Jack was very familiar with John Bunyan's *Pilgrim's Progress,* written nearly 250 years before. This was the allegorical story of a man named Christian who goes on a journey to find salvation. Jack decided that it would be interesting to write a similar sort of story about a man named John, who leaves his home in Puritania, believing it to be under the rule of a tyrant, and who, after a long journey, returns to find that he had entirely misinterpreted the situation—that the man he thought was a tyrant was, in fact, a benevolent man.

The storyline of *The Pilgrim's Regress* echoed Jack's own journey, starting life in a reasonably pious home, losing hope in God through the death of his mother and his time spent in boarding schools, and finally coming full circle back to Christian piety at Oxford.

The book was published soon after Jack finished it, but it was never a financial success. Still, Jack had immensely enjoyed the process of writing the book. Writing narrative fiction seemed to come easily to him as he wrote by hand on paper with a nibbed pen that he had to keep dipping in ink. The publishing of *The Pilgrim's Regress* represented a turning point in Jack's life. It was the first time Jack had written about a religious theme and the first time he had published anything other than poetry. These two changes transformed his writing career and set him on the long and twisting path that would lead to a mythical place he would call Narnia.

Chapter 9

Inklings

In 1933 a group called the "Inklings" began meeting together. Jack was the unofficial leader and instigator of the gathering. The group would convene in his rooms at Magdalen College on Thursday evenings and for lunch on Mondays or Fridays (or both days) in a back room of The Eagle and Child, a pub that most Oxford locals referred to as "The Bird and Baby." The purpose of the Inklings was for the members to get together to read their poems or other literary work and then give each other feedback, encouragement, and criticism. The group allowed plenty of time for general discussion and frivolity. From time to time a new person would be invited to attend the Inklings, and if the other Inklings liked the person's contribution to the conversation, they made him a permanent member.

Jack, his brother Warren, and J. R. R. Tolkien remained three of the Inklings' most regular members, along with their doctor, Robert Havard. It was fashionable for upper-class English men and women to have nicknames, and Jack started calling Dr. Havard by the initials "U. Q.," which stood for Useless Quack. The name stuck with the doctor during his entire time with the Inklings.

The Inklings served two main purposes in Jack's life. First, it gave Jack a circle of male friends whom he could spend enjoyable time with two or three times a week. Second, the meetings challenged him to continue his writing and present bits and pieces of his work for critique.

Meanwhile, Warren, who had been discharged from the army after eighteen years of service in December 1932 and now lived at The Kilns with Jack and Janie, had set himself a great task. When their father died, Jack and Warren inherited all of the Lewis and Hamilton family papers and photographs. Now Warren decided to put them all in order, write up as much information as he knew about each item, and have everything bound into volumes. When the first volume of the *Lewis Papers* was finished, Jack was impressed with the result. The volume represented hundreds of hours of tedious research, collating, reading, and writing on Warren's part.

About the time Warren finished collating the first volume of family papers, Jack began to get "fan mail" about *The Pilgrim's Regress.* Not a lot at first, just the odd letter from someone who either wanted to congratulate him on his writing style or had a specific question regarding something he'd written. Warren, who typed very slowly and laboriously, offered to answer Jack's correspondence. This was a task that would eventually turn into a full-time job.

The year 1934 started with the Lewis brothers going on their third annual walking tour. Once again they chose the Wye Valley, enjoying each other's company and the challenges of walking the countryside in midwinter. Or at least they enjoyed the countryside most of the time. On January 4, Warren wrote in his diary:

> Called at seven and got up by the light of one solitary candle, to the disquieting sound of the wind roaring in the eaves. As the daylight came, saw that in addition to the wind, a driving horizontal rain was coming out of a grey sky. However, we decided to face it, and were on the road soon after half past eight. About half a mile brought us to the point where our track left the main road, and although it was marked "Private," no one appeared to mind our using it. . . . A little further on we came upon a single plank stretched across the stream, and with some misgivings entrusted ourselves to it: J[ack] merely got his shoes wet, but it bent under my weight until the water ran over the tops of my trousers—but we were already so wet, that at that moment this seemed to produce little extra discomfort.

> We were now in really open country—nothing in front of us but a steep hill up which we began one of the most exhausting climbs I have ever undertaken: the rain beat down on us incessantly, the soggy ground was full of waterholes and subterranean rivulets, and worst of all, the higher we got, the thicker became the fog.

Eventually the brothers agreed that it was pointless to go on. They had reached a height of about seventeen hundred feet and had completely lost their bearings in the fog. They turned around and found their way down the hill until they came to an abandoned tin mine, where they took shelter. They sat together in the mine, waiting for the worst of the weather to pass. But the rain and wind did not abate, and eventually Jack and Warren headed back out into the storm, bent nearly double against the force of the wind, until they came to the town of Ponterwyd. Again Warren picked up the story in his journal:

> Here we were lucky in falling into the hands of a really kindly and intelligent landlady, who grasped the situation at once—got us as hot a bath as the house could produce at that hour of the day, and gave us beds with hot water bottles in them, while all our clothes were taken down to the kitchen to dry. Half an hour later she came up to our rooms with

> dressing gowns and offered us the use of her sitting room to have lunch in our pyjamas—and though the lunch was stewed steak, I most heartily enjoyed it.

Jack and Warren spent the rest of the day at the hotel, reading and waiting for their clothes to dry. The next day they set out again, though this time by bus to Aberystwyth, Wales, where they enjoyed rummaging around tiny bookstores and ducking into local shops and pubs. They visited the University of Wales, which was located in the town. On display in the university's library, much to Jack's delight, was a copy of Shakespeare used by Samuel Johnson in compiling *A Dictionary of the English Language* nearly two hundred years before. Words were underlined throughout the volume, and Johnson's notes were clearly visible in the margins of the pages. Warren also located in the library a copy of a paper Jack had written on medieval literature.

The inn they stayed at that night at Aberystwyth had no hot water, and both men looked forward to the homeward journey and the comforts of home that awaited them at The Kilns. Warren concluded his account of the walking tour with the words, "At Leamington we changed and had a drink under difficulties, in a very crowded refreshment room, and ultimately got to Oxford just before eight. . . . In college we found a good fire burning and a noble supper awaiting us—cold duck and salad, a tart and cheese, and a bottle of Burgundy. This put the finishing touch on a holiday which, in spite of the Ponterwyd day, I look back on as one of the very best I have ever had."

When Jack and Warren finally arrived back at The Kilns that night at around nine o'clock, they found that Janie was not well. She was now sixty-two years old and getting grumpier by the day. In fact, both Jack and Warren suspected that a lot of her "illnesses" were merely ploys to get their attention and to keep Jack, in particular, close to home to attend to her every need.

Jack, for his part, did all he could to help ease the burden of old age for Mrs. Moore—even though the more he did, the more she complained. Because trips away with Warren were about the only time Jack could justify leaving Mrs. Moore for any length of time, as soon as one tour was over he began to plan the next one. In July the two brothers took ten days off to visit family and friends in Belfast and in Glasgow, Scotland.

On Saturday, November 17, 1934, one of Jack's former students came to have tea with Jack at The Kilns. The student, Pirie Gordon, had just returned from a visit to Germany and told Jack and Warren about what was going on there. He had met with the correspondent for the *London Times* in Germany and learned of sinister things that were happening though unnoticed by most. He told of people being tortured in a secret concentration camp near Munich. Following the visit Warren noted in his journal that

Pirie Gordon "doubts if Hitler is fully aware of the cruelties which are being practiced in his name. A Herr Himmler is head of the Ogpu or whatever it is called, and is the most sinister figure in Germany. There appear to be rumours that Hitler is mentally deranged: it is common knowledge that Goering was in a private lunatic asylum at the time of the Nazi coup—his insanity being caused by excessive drug taking." Neither Jack nor Warren fully knew what to make of Pirie's observations, but the men would learn soon enough.

Life continued on at The Kilns for Jack, Warren, Janie, Maureen, and the assorted gardeners and household helpers. Warren probably found it the most difficult to live there. He resented the way Mrs. Moore treated Jack, especially since she would not allow him to work alone for more than half an hour at a time. Janie constantly interrupted Jack to fetch her a book, adjust the lamp she was reading by, or peel potatoes for dinner. Jack accepted these interruptions as part of his Christian duty, but Warren thought it was appalling that a man should be nagged that much, and he looked forward to trips away without Janie.

In January 1935 the Lewis brothers took their fourth annual walking tour, this time in the Chiltern Hills near Oxford. The weather was much kinder to them than it had been the previous year, and they both enjoyed themselves thoroughly.

When Jack returned home from the tour, he found a letter waiting for him. He slit the envelope open and read with interest that the editor of the Oxford History of English Literature series wanted him to write a volume on sixteenth-century English literature. Jack eagerly accepted the invitation.

Meanwhile, Warren was plotting a more permanent way to get some peace. In 1936 he had a twenty-foot-long motorboat built. He called it the *Bosphorus,* after a ship in his and Jack's mythical land of Boxen. Because Janie became very unhappy if Jack was out of her sight for more than twelve hours at a time, Jack was unable to use the boat. Warren, however, spent many happy hours puttering around the rivers and canals of central England. He referred to this as ditch crawling. Warren liked nothing better than to find an isolated spot on a river or canal, tie up the *Bosphorus,* and go for a long walk.

In 1937 Jack and Tolkien had another one of their life-changing conversations—a conversation that yielded spectacular results for Jack. Both men lamented the fact that they did not like the type of popular fiction that was being published at the time, and Jack issued a challenge. "Tollers, there is too little of what we really like in stories. I am afraid we shall have to try to write some ourselves."

The men agreed that Tolkien would write a book about time travel while Jack tackled one on space travel. Tolkien's attempt, titled *The Lost Road,* was never finished, but Jack worked diligently on his book idea. Jack titled his book *Out of the Silent Planet.* The storyline involved a man named Ransom, a philologist like Tolkien, who on a walking tour comes upon a house where two scientists, Weston and Devine, are planning to visit outer space, specifically a planet called Malacandra, which turns out to be Mars. Everything is ready for the voyage, except Weston and Devine need a human being to accompany them. However, Weston and Devine do not reveal their sinister plan. They believe that the inhabitants of Malacandra are fierce individuals who eat men, hence the need for an extra human on the voyage whom they could use to placate the locals upon their arrival.

Each time he finished a chapter of the book, Jack would read it aloud to the Inklings and listen to their feedback. What he heard encouraged him to keep writing. The members of the Inklings loved his story and looked forward to each new chapter.

When *Out of the Silent Planet* was finally finished, Tolkien stepped in to help Jack find a publisher for it. He sent the manuscript along with a letter from him to Stanley Unwin, who had published Tolkien's book *The Hobbit*. To Jack's dismay, Unwin rejected the book for publication. However, he forwarded the manuscript on to another publishing company, The Bodley Head, and they accepted it. In late 1938 *Out of the Silent Planet* was published and went on sale. Much to Jack's delight, it was well received by the book critics. Noted author Hugh Walpole wrote of the book, "Here is a very good book. It is of thrilling interest as a story, but it is more than that; it is a kind of poem, and it has the great virtue of improving as it goes on. It is a unique thing, full of stars, cold and heat, flowers of the planets and a sharp sardonic humour."

Already Jack saw *Out of the Silent Planet* as the first of a trilogy, and he was looking forward to writing the next two books in the series. However, as the calendar rolled over into 1939, other matters of great importance interrupted Jack's plans.

Chapter 10

War Again

For Jack 1939 started off as the seven previous years had, with a long walk through the countryside with Warren. This time the brothers chose to wander amid the Welsh marshes. Their trip also included a visit to Great Malvern, where they had both attended school. It was a poignant time for both Jack and Warren as they recalled times gone by. It was made even more poignant by the fact that Europe seemed once again poised on the brink of war—as it had been in 1914 during Jack's last term at Great Malvern.

The walking trip through the Welsh marshes presented an interesting challenge for the Lewis brothers, since it snowed every day. But despite the discomfort the snow brought to their walk, Jack and Warren were entranced by the magical spell a blanket of snow cast over the landscape. The scene was one that Jack would later vividly recapture at the start of one of his books.

When Jack and Warren finally returned to The Kilns, they braced themselves for what lay ahead. If Germany, under Adolf Hitler's leadership, did declare war, Warren was sure that he would be recalled to active service. He dreaded the thought, as he did not feel he had the psychological strength to return to the battlefield and watch his fellow soldiers being slaughtered.

Jack, on the other hand, was sure that he would not be called up. He still had pieces of shrapnel embedded in his chest from World War I that would make him unfit for active duty. But the idea of sitting around while England needed men to go and fight did not settle well with him. In the end, however, all he or anyone else in England could do was wait and watch as the storm clouds of war continued to gather over Europe.

While they waited, Jack embarked on writing a new book. The book was nonfiction, an exploration—or apology—for why God allows His children, whom He loves, to endure pain. *The Problem of Pain* was a short book, just forty thousand words, commissioned by a small London publishing house. Jack enjoyed the challenge of writing it, especially since he got to write in a different voice—not that of an Oxford don or a fiction writer but of a lawyer arguing a case. Before Jack was able to finish the book, however, war broke out.

On September 30, 1938, the governments of Britain and France had concluded a pact with Germany whereby the Nazis were allowed to keep Sudetenland, the narrow strip of land they had annexed from Czechoslovakia. In return, Germany promised that it would not invade any more territory in Europe. Upon returning to England after negotiating the pact, British prime minister Neville Chamberlain declared it to be "peace in our time." But on March 15, 1939, the Nazis shattered that peace and the pact when they invaded the rest of Czechoslovakia.

Two months later, Adolf Hitler signed a pact with Italy agreeing that each country would support the other if war were to break out in Europe. And on August 23, 1939, the Nazis signed a ten-year nonaggression pact with Joseph Stalin, the Russian dictator. Germany then demanded the return of the city of Danzig (Gdansk) and the strip of land that linked East Prussia to Germany, territory the Germans had lost to Poland at the end of World War I.

In response to the Nazis' threats and demands on Poland, Britain signed an agreement that it would come to Poland's aid if the Germans attacked the country. And that is just what the Nazis did. On September 1, 1939, Germany annexed Danzig, and German troops poured across the border and invaded Poland, unleashing a blistering and devastating air attack against the country.

In the early morning hours of Sunday, September 3, the British prime minister issued an ultimatum to Germany: immediately cease the invasion of Poland or face all-out war with Great Britain. The Nazis ignored the ultimatum, and at 11:15 AM Prime Minister Chamberlain interrupted regularly scheduled radio broadcasts to announce to the population that Great Britain was officially at war with Germany. Twelve minutes later the air-raid sirens in London began to wail. It was only a test, but it brought home to everyone the reality of the situation. Britain's Commonwealth allies, Canada, Australia, and New Zealand, also declared war on Germany.

With the country at war, the British government began mobilizing its troops to fight the Germans, and on September 4, 1939, Warren Lewis, now forty-five years old, was recalled to active service. He was sent to the army base at Catterick, Yorkshire, where he was given training in the latest innovations in war transportation and prepared himself to once again go and fight the Germans. Warren was also promoted to the rank of major and posted with the British Expeditionary Force to Le Havre, France.

The early stage of this mobilization was a time of great confusion in England. The government declared that it would take over Magdalen College. It took Jack two days to pack up all his books and lug them down to the basement. Then shortly afterward the government decided that Magdalen College would remain open, and Jack had to carry all of his books back upstairs to his office and rearrange them.

In London residents were required to carry gas masks with them at all times, and people busied themselves filling sandbags to barricade buildings in case the Germans began bombing the city from the air with the same ferocity as they were bombing Poland. Barrage balloons also floated above the city as a trap for enemy airplanes. In fact, the fear of impending air attacks by the Germans against London was so great that the government decided to evacuate the children from the city. All traffic into London was stopped, and all roads leading in and out of the city were made one-way roads out to aid in the evacuation of the city.

Like most other households in the English countryside, Jack and Janie felt obliged to open the doors at The Kilns to some of the displaced children. Although she was now sixty-seven years old, Janie loved children and was eager to help in any way she could. Jack, on the other hand, was a confirmed bachelor who was happy to admit that he was fairly clueless about how children thought and behaved. Nonetheless, in early September 1939, three teenage girls who were evacuated from a convent school in London came to stay with the family at The Kilns.

Thankfully, the advent of war provided one positive aspect for Jack. Charles Williams, whom Jack had met several times, moved to Oxford at the beginning of the war when Oxford University Press, where Charles was an editor, relocated there from London to escape the threat of German bombardment. As well as being an editor, Charles was an accomplished novelist, and he was soon a regular member of the Inklings. He and Jack quickly became close friends, spending hours together talking about writing. Jack's friendship with Charles also filled the void Jack felt at Warren's departure to the war.

Once Warren arrived in France, Jack constantly worried about his brother's safety. The Nazis were proving to be a very brutal and merciless foe, and Jack was scared that Warren would be killed at their hands. He noted his fears in the lines to a poem he scribbled in a notebook:

> How can I ask thee Father to defend
> In peril of war my brother's hand to-day?

Although Jack did not like war, he firmly believed that Adolf Hitler and his troops had to be stopped in their tracks before they wreaked even more havoc on Europe and the rest of the world. Thinking of ways in which he could help the war effort, he tried to enlist as an instructor of cadets, but he was turned down for this position. However, it was suggested that he might be useful in the Ministry of Information. But when Jack investigated this opportunity, he discovered that it would involve writing propaganda and lies, and he decided that this was not the job for him. Instead, Jack signed up as a member of the Oxford City Home Guard Battalion, a group of part-time soldiers who were to be on the alert for German aircraft and confirm if they dropped bombs or invaded the land by parachute.

Jack's first job as part of the home guard was to help the local people prepare against possible German bombing by aircraft. The task involved completely blacking out the entire city at night so that German navigators would not be able to see the city from the air. To do this, every house had to have thick blackout curtains draped across its windows so that not a glimmer of light showed through them. Also, cars could no longer travel at night, since they were not allowed to use their headlights. This rule became even easier to enforce when gas began to be severely rationed. With no gas, most people either sold their cars or locked them up in their garages and instead walked or used what limited public transportation was available during the day.

Jack enjoyed his responsibility with the home guard, and in a letter to Warren in France he wrote about being on duty the night before. He had rendezvoused at Luke Street,

> eating my sandwiches on the way. . . . I was with two men much younger than myself . . . both very nice and intelligent and neither too talkative nor too silent. One is allowed to smoke and I was pleased to find out that our tour of duty included a quite prolonged soak on the verandah of a college pavilion—a pleasant spot, looking out over broad playing fields on a mild but windy night of sufficient starlight and some light clouds—with the occasional interest of a train trundling past. . . . Three hours passed surprisingly quickly, and if it hadn't been for the bother of lugging a rifle about all the time I should have said that

> pleasure distinctly predominated. . . . We broke off at 4:30 and after a really beautiful walk back through an empty and twilight Oxford I was in bed by 5.

As part of the preparations for a possible German invasion or bombing from the air, dugouts and bomb shelters had to be built. Jack and the gardener busied themselves creating a large bomb shelter in the garden at The Kilns.

With these preparations taken care of, Jack waited anxiously to see what the Germans would do next and what course the war would take.

Chapter 11

A Radio Star

For the first few months after Britain declared war on Germany, apart from a few small skirmishes, very little action took place on the western front in France. These months of the war were thus referred to as the "Phony War." Instead, Adolf Hitler concentrated his efforts on subduing Poland and tightening his control over the other areas he had invaded and annexed. But all that began to change in April 1940, when the Germans invaded Denmark and then Norway. British soldiers were sent to Norway to help beat back the invasion, but there was no stopping the German advance. The troops were withdrawn in May, and Norway fell into Nazi hands. At the same time, the Germans invaded the Netherlands, Luxembourg, and Belgium. These countries tried to resist the invasion, but the powerful German military quickly swept such opposition aside and conquered the countries.

By mid-May 1940 the Germans began their push into France, surging through the Ardennes region and advancing rapidly north to capture Calais. In the process the combined Allied forces of British, French, and Belgian soldiers were trapped against the coastline on the French-Belgian border and were slowly forced back toward the French town of Dunkirk.

The news that the Germans had trapped so many of their soldiers in northern France was a bitter blow to the British people. Jack was particularly concerned when he learned that among those trapped was the British Expeditionary Force, in which Warren was serving.

As Jack fretted about Warren's safety, on May 22 Winston Churchill, who twelve days earlier had succeeded Neville Chamberlain as the new British prime minister, set in motion Operation Dynamo under the command of Vice Admiral Bertram Ramsay. The purpose of the operation was to muster as many ships and small boats, both civilian and military, as possible and use them to cross the English Channel to France and rescue the trapped Allied soldiers.

From May 29 to June 3, 1940, a ceaseless flotilla of ships and boats began crossing to France and plucking soldiers to safety from the beaches of Dunkirk. The boats endured punishing bombing from the German Luftwaffe (air force), but by the time the operation ended, 338,226 troops had been ferried to safety in England aboard approximately seven hundred different vessels that took part in the operation.

Early in June, Jack received word that Warren had been safely evacuated from Dunkirk to Wenvoe Camp, in Cardiff, Wales, and was in the hospital recovering from an illness. Jack heaved a sigh of relief, happy to have his brother back in Great Britain, even if the country was still under threat.

In July 1940, while listening to a rather boring sermon at Holy Trinity Church in Headington Quarry, Jack was struck with an interesting idea for a book. He began to wonder what would happen if readers could eavesdrop on a series of conversations between an elderly, experienced devil and a young devil just entrusted with his first "patient" to derail from the Christian faith. As Jack pondered the idea, two characters marched into his head, a senior devil named Screwtape and his nephew Wormwood, a very inexperienced Tempter.

Jack's mind quickly darted down lines of reasoning, examining the various ways in which Christians lose their faith. Jack thought, for example, about prayer and how a Christian asks God to answer a particular prayer—for patience, for instance. If God does not seem to answer the prayer, it is easy for a person to believe that God does not exist, and if God does answer the prayer, it is easy for the person to twist that fact into thinking that he or she can solve his or her own problems through a kind of self-hypnosis. This was the kind of issue that Jack envisaged the senior devil discussing with the junior devil.

The book, which Jack initially called *As One Devil to Another,* took shape quickly. Jack decided to write it in the form of letters from Screwtape to Wormwood, giving advice on the difficult situations Wormwood faced as he tried to tempt his "patient" to sin. Jack's idea was to entertain Christians and at the same time plant seeds in their minds as to how Satan works in small, subtle ways to counteract God's goodness.

Meanwhile Warren, who was still weak from his illness, was transferred to the Officer Reserve on August 16 and sent home to Oxford to join the 6th Oxford City Home Guard Battalion. His assignments included cruising the upper Thames River in his motorboat *Bosphorus* and boating along little-used canals, checking that all of the buildings along the banks were completely blacked out. Warren's new duty became more important than ever when, in August 1940, Hitler unleashed a massive bombing campaign against Great Britain, in what would become known as the Battle of Britain. Day and night, wave after wave of German bombers flew over the country, dropping their deadly cargo on the English countryside. As well as bombing London and other British cities, the bombers targeted Royal Air Force (RAF) bases in an attempt to destroy the RAF in advance of a German invasion of Great Britain.

The British, however, were not so easily defeated. Fighter planes from the Royal Air Force put up a gallant fight, shooting down and destroying hundreds of German bombers, so many, in fact, that the Germans soon stopped their daytime bombing runs over

England and resorted to bombing London by night. The decisive British victory in the sky meant that Hitler was eventually forced to abandon his plans to invade England.

Back at The Kilns, Jack was overjoyed to have his brother home again, especially since Maureen Moore was getting married the week after he arrived. Both Jack and Warren knew Maureen's husband-to-be, who was director of music at Worksop College.

By February 1941 the Battle of Britain was well over, and a stack of thirty-one letters from Screwtape sat on Jack's desktop—each one addressing a different tactic of the devil. With the letters complete, Jack decided to first publish them individually. He sent them off to his favorite newspaper, the *Guardian,* a weekly paper owned by the Church of England. The editor of the *Guardian* liked the letters and offered Jack sixty-two pounds to publish them all. Jack accepted the offer, and instead of keeping the money, he asked that the editor send it to a charity fund for widows of Church of England clergymen.

As the letters were published one by one, they became an instant success—so popular, in fact, that the *Guardian* soon had to double the number of newspapers it printed each week. By the time the fourth letter reached the public, a publisher named Geoffrey Bles was interested in buying the rights to the letters and publishing them in book form. After a little negotiation, Jack signed a contract and waited for the book, to be titled *The Screwtape Letters,* to be published by Centenary Press.

Meanwhile, Jack received a letter from Dr. James Welch, the director of religious broadcasting at the British Broadcasting Corporation (BBC). Dr. Welch had read some of Jack's work and wanted to know if Jack had anything that he would like to prepare to read on the radio. At first Jack laughed off the idea. He hated nothing more than the radio, much preferring to read a book or listen to a record on the gramophone. However, he soon realized that as a result of the merciless German bombing of England, morale in the country was low and many people who would not ordinarily do so were thinking about matters of life and death. He wrote back to Dr. Welch and offered to give a fifteen-minute talk each Wednesday night during the month of August 1941.

The talks, titled "Right and Wrong: A Clue to the Meaning of the Universe" and broadcast live from the BBC studios in London, were a huge success. Jack soon found himself overwhelmed by letters from listeners. Some of those who wrote wanted advice regarding specific situations, while others wanted to share their theological views with Jack. Everyone, it seemed, was stunned that an Oxford don could attract so much attention. Dr. Welch suggested that Jack take another fifteen minutes on the air to read and then answer some of the listeners' questions. The hope was that this would stem the tide of letters that continued to arrive at the BBC and were forwarded on to Jack. Predictably, the opposite occurred. The more personally interested Jack appeared to be in the opinions and questions of his listeners, the more people wrote to him. Jack was glad to have Warren back at The Kilns, where he took on the task of answering the bulk of the letters in his methodical way.

Eventually Jack gave seven different series of lectures on the BBC around the themes of what Christians believe and how they should live in society. The transcripts of his first two series were published together in July 1942 under the title *Broadcast Talks*. The book became an immediate bestseller. In 1954 the texts from all seven of the lecture series were gathered together and published in a single book titled *Mere Christianity*.

Hearing what a competent and compelling speaker Jack was on the radio, the chaplain-in-chief of the Royal Air Force, the Reverend Maurice Edwards, approached Jack about undertaking a speaking tour of air force bases in Great Britain, where Jack could encourage the troops in the war effort. Jack was not convinced that he could be of much use in that sphere, but he remembered from his time in the army during World War I how frightening it was to be a young man poised to enter battle. So he agreed to do what he could.

Soon Jack was spending most weekends traversing England by train to various RAF stations, where sometimes only a small group of men gathered to hear him speak and at other times hundreds of men crowded together to hear him talk. But whether the group was big or small, the men were all eager to hear something that would lift their spirits. In December 1941 Jack wrote to his friend Arthur Greeves, outlining how he had spent his winter holidays:

> All through the Vacation I was going round lecturing to the R.A.F.—away for 2 or 3 days at a time and then home for 2 or 3 days. I had never realized how tiring perpetual traveling is (specially in crowded trains). One felt all the time as if one had just played a game of football—aching all over. None the less I had some interesting times and saw some beautiful country. Perthshire, and all the country between Aberystwyth and Shrewsbury, and Cumberland, are what chiefly stuck in my mind. It also gave me the chance in many places to see and smell the sea and hear the sound of gulls again, which otherwise I would have been pining for.

Sometimes Warren would accompany Jack on legs of his speaking tour, but both brothers were careful to be back in Oxford for Monday nights to attend the weekly meeting of a new club. The club was the Oxford Socratic Club, and Jack had been appointed its president. The purpose of the Socratic Club was to be an "open forum for the discussion of the intellectual difficulties connected with religion and with Christianity in particular." Each Monday night a lively group of students and teachers from Oxford, both atheists and Christians, gathered together to listen to various speakers from across the religious spectrum and then logically explore what had been said, paying close attention to any holes in a person's argument or reasoning. Jack was particularly gifted at presenting the intellectual case for Christianity and for shooting down the arguments of atheists.

In his "spare time," Jack set about the task of writing the second novel in his science-fiction trilogy. This book was titled *Perelandra.*

Meanwhile, in February 1942, *The Screwtape Letters* was published. At first only two thousand copies of the book were printed, but these were sold even before they came off the press. In the end the book was reprinted eight times during its first year of publication. *The Screwtape Letters* was even published in the United States.

Although Jack cringed at the idea, he was now a celebrity, and letters from admirers flowed in. This was in addition to the fame he had garnered from his radio talks on the BBC. At the time *The Screwtape Letters* was published, Jack was delivering a series of talks titled "What Christians Believe." This series was so popular that he quickly prepared another, this time exploring Christian behavior. Each time Jack delivered a new series of talks on the BBC, he became more popular and received more complimentary reviews. One reviewer wrote:

> Mr. Lewis is that rare thing—being a born broadcaster: born to the manner as well as the matter. He neither buttonholes you nor

> bombards you; there is no false intimacy and no false eloquence. He approaches you directly, as a rational person only to be persuaded by reason. He is confident and yet humble in his possession and propagation of the truth. He is helped by a speaking voice of great charm and style of manifest sincerity.

Jack chose to speak on Christian behavior mainly because that is what he was being tested on at home at The Kilns. The biggest test came in the form of Mrs. Moore, who was now a very grumpy and demanding old woman. Janie's brother had gone insane several years earlier, and as Jack watched Janie descend into stranger and stranger behavior, he wondered whether she too was following her brother on the road to insanity. Janie had no tolerance for ration cards, blacking out the house at night, or the Lewis brothers' midnight patrols. In fact, she treated every inconvenience as if it had been planned just to annoy her. Jack needed all the patience and kindness he could muster to continue looking after her.

Several of the girls who had evacuated from London and were billeted at The Kilns worked hard to keep Mrs. Moore from becoming too agitated. One of these girls in particular, sixteen-year-old June Flewett, had an intuitive sense of what needed to be done to calm the household. June spent many hundreds of hours doing menial tasks to Mrs. Moore's exacting standards. As Jack and Warren watched June, they realized what an extraordinary young woman she was. Jack decided that one day he would model a character in one of his books after her.

The war with Germany and her allies dragged on. At first, after the evacuation of troops from Dunkirk and the subsequent German bombing of Great Britain from the air, the mood of the country was gloomy. In fact, everyone in England was certain that a German invasion was imminent. Jack, too, was so convinced an invasion was near that one day when he remembered that his old officer's revolver from World War I was in his bedside drawer, he slipped the weapon into his pocket and walked to Magdalen Bridge. He threw the revolver into the river, fearing that the invading Germans would shoot him and everyone else at The Kilns if they were to find the gun.

German submarines were busy bombing merchant ships carrying much-needed goods to England, thus creating severe shortages of some foods and supplies and leading to a tightening of the rationing system.

Slowly the mood began to change. After Japanese airplanes bombed the U.S. Pacific Fleet at Pearl Harbor, Hawaii, in December 1941, the United States entered the war. Soon fresh-faced American soldiers were showing up in England, where their appearance began to lift people's spirits.

After so many apparent German victories in the war, the tide began to turn. In North Africa Allied forces beat back the Germans and Italians and eventually began invading Italy. And because they were unable to subdue the Soviets, having to abort their invasion of Russia due to harsh weather and the tenacity of the Soviet defenders, the Germans were now fighting the war on two fronts, stretching their resources to the limits.

By the time 1944 dawned, it was becoming obvious that the Allied forces would eventually defeat the Germans. It was just a matter of time. Then on June 6, 1944, D-day, a massive Allied invasion of France began on the beaches of Normandy. At first the Germans put up stiff resistance, but as the Allies kept invading, the Germans began to pull back.

As he read accounts of the Allied advances in France against the Germans, Jack knew it would not be long until the war would finally be over. He looked forward to the time when Great Britain and the rest of Europe and the world could put the madness of war behind them once and for all.

Chapter 12

A Children's Fairy Tale

May 8, 1945, was a day no one in England at the time would ever forget. The day before, Germany had surrendered unconditionally to her Allied opponents. The war was over! Euphoria broke out in the streets. People hugged each other and wept for joy. People partied. The Union Jack fluttered proudly from flagpoles. The people of Great Britain had weathered the darkest days of the war, when it seemed certain that the Nazis were about to invade their country. They had persevered against the odds, and now, with the help of her Allies, Great Britain had prevailed. Adolf Hitler's Germany had been smashed into surrender.

Like everyone else in the country, Jack was relieved that the war had finally ended. He and

Warren were alive, the rhythm of their lives largely unaltered except for their civil-defense duties and the inconveniences of worn-out shoes and a limited amount of food to eat.

Although the war in Europe was over, people realized that it would take years for the continent to fully recover from the ravages of that war. For one thing, rationing would continue for quite some time. However, few English people realized at the time the ongoing sacrifices they would have to make. Shortages of food continued until even potatoes, a staple of the English diet, had to be rationed. Warren complained of going to bed hungry and waking up hungry.

While the Inklings had continued to meet throughout the war, the flow of the group was often interrupted by the comings and goings of group members. Now, Jack hoped, the group could get back into full swing. Within two weeks of the end of the war, however, Jack's friend and fellow writer Charles Williams from Oxford University Press died suddenly. The day after the end of the war, Charles was gripped with stomach pains and checked himself into the local hospital. His condition was not thought to be serious. The next week, after an Inklings meeting, Jack went to visit Charles, only to be told that his friend had just died. After making it through the entire war without suffering any personal loss, Jack was devastated by the sudden death of his friend. He expressed his feelings in a letter to another friend, a nun named Sister Penelope:

> You will have heard of the death of my dearest friend, Charles Williams, and, no doubt, prayed for him. For me too, it has been, and is, a great loss. But not at all a dejecting one. It has greatly increased my faith. Death has done nothing to my idea of him, but he has done—oh, I can't say what—to my idea of death. It has made the next world much more real and palpable.

The next world probably seemed more real to Jack for another reason too. Jack was anxiously awaiting the publication of his latest book titled *The Great Divorce: A Dream.* The fourteen chapters of the book had been published one by one in the *Guardian* between November 1944 and April 1945 and then gathered together into a single volume that was published in November 1945. The book recounted an imaginary journey of a group of people from hell to view the wonders of heaven. It was written in Jack's usual clear and concise style. More than anything Jack tried to write so that anyone could understand what he wrote, noting in a letter to a critic, "Any fool can write learned language. The vernacular is the real test. If you can't turn your faith into it, then either you don't understand it, or you don't believe it."

Whenever Jack wrote on religious themes, his goal was always to make Christianity accessible to as large a number of common folk as possible. Of course he was tested on this at home. Despite the popularity of Jack's Christian writing, Mrs. Moore still deeply resented the fact that Jack had become a Christian, and she refused to have anything to do with religion herself. It was not surprising, then, that a character very much like Janie Moore appeared in *The Great Divorce.*

After completing this book, Jack began work on a more intense theological book called *Miracles: A Preliminary Study.* Meanwhile, the publication of *The Great Divorce* brought Jack to the attention of serious theologians. In early 1946 the University of St. Andrews in Scotland bestowed a great honor on him. The school awarded him a doctor of divinity degree, making him Dr. C. S. Lewis.

Jack squirmed at the idea of all the attention, but he did enjoy the trip north to receive the degree. Warren accompanied him, and the two brothers spent a few days at the seaside in Scotland. It reminded them of their summer vacations at the beach at Castlerock as children back in Ireland.

While Jack was away in Scotland receiving his honorary degree, Mrs. Moore's health deteriorated further, to the point where she could hardly get out of bed. However, this did not stop her from yelling instructions from her upstairs bedroom. Her illness had become a burden to Jack, leaving him feeling guilty if he stayed away from The Kilns for a whole day, much less overnight.

To make matters worse, things were not going well with the Inklings either. After Charles Williams's death, the number of men regularly attending the group began to dwindle. J. R. R. Tolkien continued to come and to read pieces from a book he had been writing for years now about a magical place filled with hobbits and elves, but the personal relationship between him and Jack was becoming more distant. No one knows for sure all of the reasons that caused this cooling in their friendship, but one reason had to do with the volume Jack had just completed for the Oxford History of English Literature. The book was on English literature during the sixteenth century, and in it Jack had fallen into some of his old Protestant Irish habits when categorizing Catholics. He referred to them as papists instead of Catholics, and he tended to play up the role of early Protestant pioneers at the expense of gifted Catholic theologians, writers, and thinkers. All of this struck a sour note with Tolkien, who saw Jack's new volume as anti-Catholic. Tolkien took the matter personally, creating a wedge that slowly began to push the two men apart.

The book *Miracles: A Preliminary Study* was published right about the same time that a book by Bishop Barnes titled *Rise of Christianity* was published. The two books took totally different views on miracles. Jack argued that miracles occur when God decides to intervene in human affairs. The bishop argued that there is no such thing as a real miracle, but that what we see as a miracle has a natural cause that we do not yet understand.

Both books sold well upon their release, and many Christians bought them both so that they could decide for themselves what they thought about miracles. Of course, it was natural that the Oxford Socratic Club would become engaged in the debate. One night Jack found himself arguing for his point of view against a well-known Catholic philosopher named Elizabeth Anscombe. The meeting took place in February 1948. Elizabeth came prepared to debate Jack, particularly regarding chapter three of his book. Her response to Jack's argument for miracles revolved around her argument that naturalism is self-refuting.

The debate was lively. Elizabeth was sharp and insightful in her critique of Jack's argument, leaving Jack at times stumbling for words as he responded to the points she made. Some of those attending the packed meeting said that it was the liveliest debate ever held at the Socratic Club. Those in attendance were at odds as to who won the exchange. Some said that Jack came out the winner, while others thought Elizabeth was clearly on top. Jack for his part was not sure. He was shaken by the whole experience and wondered just how much could be achieved in advancing Christianity through intellectual argument alone. In light of some of Elizabeth's criticisms, Jack revised chapter three of his book for future editions.

Despite his experience at the Oxford Socratic Club, by now Jack was one of the most famous Christians in Great Britain. He was so influential that he was invited to join a group of archbishops to discuss the future of the Church of England. Jack attended the meetings, though it was difficult for him to leave The Kilns. By way of explanation in accepting the invitation he wrote, "My mother [Mrs. Moore] is old and infirm, we have little and uncertain help, and I never know when I can, even for a day, get away from my duties as a nurse and domestic servant (there are psychological as well as material difficulties in my house). But I will come if I possibly can."

The situation at home at The Kilns was made more difficult because Warren nursed an intense dislike for Mrs. Moore and often coped with the stress at home by drinking too much.

While Jack dealt with the constant stress that now inhabited The Kilns, he returned to an idea he had first visited during the war—an idea for a fairy tale for children. The notion had started as the germ of an idea long before that. When Jack was sixteen years old, an image had popped into his head. It was of a faun walking upright through a snowy wood, carrying an umbrella in one arm and parcels in the other, nothing more than that. But the image was so vivid that Jack determined to use it one day in something he wrote. Now the image had come back to him, and he decided to see what he could do with it.

As Jack thought the concept through, he realized that he had spent little time with children throughout his life. There was Maureen, of course, who was twelve years old when he first met her. There were also the girls who had come to stay at The Kilns after being evacuated from London. At the time, Jack had written to Warren, "Our schoolgirls (i.e. evacuees) have arrived and all seem to be very nice, unaffected creatures and all most flatteringly delighted with their surroundings. They are fond of animals, which is a good thing." Then a couple of weeks later he continued his commentary. "I have said that the children are 'nice,' and so they are. But modern children are poor creatures. They keep coming to Maureen and asking 'What shall we do now?'"

Jack's mind began to churn with ideas. What could he possibly do with an umbrella-carrying faun running through a snowy wood, and a group of evacuee children who were bored living with an elderly couple? Soon Jack had the hazy outline of a story:

> This book is about four children whose names are Ann, Martin, Rose and Peter. But it is most about Peter who was the youngest. They all had to go away from London suddenly because of Air Raids, and because Father, who was in the Army, had gone off to the War and Mother was doing some kind of war work. They were sent to stay with a kind of relation of Mother's who was a very old Professor who lived by himself in the country.

One day, soon after coming up with this rough outline, Jack sat staring at the large, wooden wardrobe his grandfather had built and intricately carved years before. *Perhaps,* he thought, *I might be able to work that into the story as well.*

Around the same time, Jack began having a recurring nightmare involving a lion—in particular, a large male lion with a bushy mane. Jack gave the lion a name—Aslan—and began searching for a way to work him into the story too.

Jack also began thinking back to the stories of Edith Nesbit that he had read as a boy. He particularly called to mind her trilogy of stories: *Railway Children, The Phoenix and the Carpet,* and *The Story of the Amulet.* He remembered how in *The Story of the Amulet* some children discovered an amulet that was able to transport them back in time to strange new worlds. And so Jack began to integrate some of the ideas from these stories into his thinking.

While Jack was busy teasing out his idea for a children's fairy tale, Roger Green, a former student and now a friend of Jack's, asked him if he would read a manuscript of a story that he'd written for children. Jack found the manuscript, titled *The Wood That Time Forgot,* to be very exciting, and Roger's story inspired him to keep on writing his own story. Sometimes images from Roger's manuscript or pictures from Jack's past would pop into Jack's head as he wrote. At other times Jack made things up as he went along. He described his own writing process this way:

> With me the process is much more like bird-watching than like either talking or building. I see pictures. Some of the pictures have a common flavour, almost a common smell, which groups them together. Keep quiet and watch and they will begin joining themselves up. If you were very lucky (I have never been so lucky as all that) a whole group might join themselves so consistently that there you had a complete story; without doing anything yourself. But more often (in my experience

> always) there are gaps. Then at last you have to do some deliberate inventing.

The story of *The Lion, the Witch and the Wardrobe* was beginning to take shape. It involved the Pevensie children—Peter, Susan, Edmund, and Lucy—whose names had changed from the Ann, Martin, Rose, and Peter that Jack had originally conceived for them. The children are evacuated from London and go to stay in the country with Professor Kirke and his bossy housekeeper. The Pevensies become so bored in their new surroundings that they decide to play hide-and-seek in the old professor's home. In the process Lucy discovers an ancient wardrobe in the attic and climbs in to hide. She pushes herself to the back of the pile of fur coats hanging in the wardrobe and tumbles into a strange, snowy land, where she encounters a faun hurrying along carrying an umbrella and some parcels. The faun, whose name is Mr. Tumnus, stops and talks to Lucy and takes her back to his place to have a cup of tea. Lucy spends all afternoon at the faun's house before he leads her back to the lamppost that marks the entrance to the back of the wardrobe, the portal to this magical world the reader learns is called Narnia.

Although she thinks she has been away all afternoon, when she emerges from the wardrobe, Lucy discovers that only minutes have passed, and her older brothers and sister refuse to believe that she has spent the afternoon with a faun in a strange, cold land.

As Jack wrote on, he slowly arranged circumstances in his story until finally all the Pevensie children were in Narnia. There Edmund is deceived by the White Witch, who entices him with his favorite treat—Turkish delight—to betray his brother and sisters. Eventually Edmund's eyes are opened to the treachery of the White Witch, but not until it's too late to stop the high price his betrayal will exact on the inhabitants of Narnia and, in particular, Aslan the lion. However, by the time the story winds toward its close, Peter, Susan, Edmund, and Lucy have all proved themselves in battle and in service to the inhabitants of Narnia. The four of them are crowned as kings and queens of Narnia and in so doing, fulfill an ancient prophecy, the very thing the White Witch was trying to keep from happening. After many years of ruling over Narnia from Cair Paravel, the capital, the Pevensie children take a long horse ride through the countryside and come upon an overgrown lamppost. The sight of the lamppost calls to mind a distant memory of another place and time. As they search about, Peter, Susan, Edmund, and Lucy stumble into the back of the wardrobe and arrive in the attic room of Professor Kirke's home on earth, where, despite what seems to them like an absence of many years in Narnia, only a short time has passed on earth from the time they entered the wardrobe.

The story came together quickly, and when it was finished in March 1949, Jack wondered whether he had created anything that anyone would want to read. He showed his manuscript to J. R. R. Tolkien, who, despite the growing rift in their relationship, was still his most trusted editorial friend.

The result was devastating. Tolkien hated the story. He believed that a person should not mix various cultural mythologies and complained that there were far too many types of characters in the story. Some of them, like the White Witch and the nymphs, came from Greek myths; knights were from the Middle Ages; and then there was Father Christmas, based on a church bishop, and two talking beavers who sounded like they were friends of Beatrix Potter's Peter Rabbit.

Jack argued that the jumbled cast of characters lived happily together in his imagination, but Tolkien replied that they certainly could not live in his imagination, at least not at the same time. Tolkien shook his head sadly and told Jack that if he could find a publisher, this book would stand out as an embarrassment to him and the entire group of Inklings.

Jack found the criticism from his old friend hard to take, partly because he had some doubts of his own about the story and partly because all along he had been encouraging Tollers to complete the book he had been writing now for several years. Tolkien called the book *The Lord of the Rings,* and Jack was sure that if Tolkien ever succeeded in finishing it, the book would be a masterpiece.

Following Tolkien's negative response, Jack was tempted to put the manuscript for his story back on the shelf and forget about it. And he may well have, except that he gave a copy to Dr. Havard, who let his daughter Mary Clare read it. Mary Clare loved the story, causing Jack to realize that he had written the story for children after all, and not for intellectual adults like Tolkien.

This positive feedback emboldened Jack to ask Roger Green to read his manuscript and see whether he thought it had any merit. Roger very much liked what he read, though he had to agree with Tolkien that Father Christmas seemed very out of place in the story.

Jack thought about Roger's remarks, but in the end he insisted on leaving Father Christmas where he was in the story. However, Jack did take Roger's other piece of advice. He sent the manuscript for *The Lion, the Witch and the Wardrobe* off to his publisher, Geoffrey Bles, and waited nervously to see whether he concurred with Tolkien that the story was nothing but an embarrassment, or whether he liked it and would consider publishing it.

Before he received a reply from his publisher, however, the stress of his writing and teaching schedule and the burden of caring for Janie Moore caught up with fifty-year-old Jack. In June 1949 Jack collapsed and had to be rushed to the hospital by ambulance. He had a high fever, and his glands were swollen. Dr. Havard administered penicillin shots to Jack every three hours. Jack spent more than a week in the hospital recuperating.

When Dr. Havard explained to Jack that his condition was a result of his becoming run-down by the stress of all his responsibilities at home and at the university, Warren became incensed. Although he could not do much about Jack's responsibilities at Magdalen College, he stormed home to The Kilns to do something about the stressful situation there. He explained the reason for Jack's collapse to Mrs. Moore and demanded that she leave his brother in peace for a month so that he could make a full recovery. Shocked by Warren's fury at her, Janie Moore reluctantly agreed and, for a while, stopped making incessant demands of Jack when he returned home from the hospital.

Chapter 13

Chronicling Narnia

As Jack recuperated at The Kilns, he waited anxiously to hear from his publisher regarding *The Lion, the Witch and the Wardrobe.* Finally a letter from Geoffrey Bles arrived. In the letter Geoffrey confided to Jack that he was less than excited about *The Lion, the Witch and the Wardrobe.* He doubted that such a book would sell. Like Tolkien, he thought that its publication might even hurt Jack's literary reputation and the sales of his other books. But Geoffrey did not dismiss the story outright as had Tolkien. Instead, he suggested that if Jack wanted to have it published, it should be the first in a series of children's books.

Although these comments from his publisher were less than the ringing endorsement he had hoped for, nonetheless Jack was encouraged by them. Geoffrey would publish *The Lion, the Witch and the Wardrobe* if it were part of a series of books. That in turn sent Jack back to Narnia, the imaginary world that was now alive in his imagination as Boxen and Animal-Land had been when he was a child. Jack began thinking about other stories that could occur in Narnia. Eventually he settled on writing the story of the beginnings of Narnia and the first humans to visit the place. He hoped in the process to explain where the lamppost in Narnia and the wardrobe in Professor Kirke's attic came from.

Jack called the new story he embarked upon *Polly and Digory,* after its two main characters, Polly Plummer and Digory Kirke. All went well with the story until Jack introduced the character of Mrs. Lefay, Digory's godmother and a woman skilled in the ways of magic. Something about this character didn't feel right to Jack, and his writing began to bog down. When he read to Roger Green what he had written so far, Roger confirmed Jack's feelings about the character.

Unsure how to correct the wrong turn the story had taken, Jack decided to abandon *Polly and Digory* and instead start in on a new story. This story he called *Drawn into Narnia,* and Jack busily set to writing it. The opening line read, "Once there were four children whose names were Peter, Susan, Edmund, and Lucy, and it has been told in another book called *The Lion, the Witch and the Wardrobe* how they had a remarkable adventure."

At the start of the story, the Pevensie children are waiting for the train that will take them back to boarding school, when they are suddenly and surprisingly pulled back into Narnia. In Narnian time a thousand years has passed since they ruled over the land from the capital Cair Paravel. The children had ruled during a Golden Age, but now Narnia is a very different place, where a state of civil war exists. The animals, trees, and dwarfs of old Narnia have been banished by the Telmarines, people from our world who found their way into Narnia and have taken it over. Prince Caspian, the rightful heir to the throne of Narnia, wants to assume the throne that is his and return Narnia to the "old" ways, but he is thwarted by his uncle Miraz, a despot who calls himself the Lord Protector and who is actively hunting down his nephew in order to kill him. But when Prince Caspian blows the horn given to Susan Pevensie in *The Lion, the Witch and the Wardrobe,* the Pevensie children are magically called back to Narnia to aid the prince in his struggle. Along with Prince Caspian, Peter, Susan, Edmund, and Lucy unite all those true to the old ways of Narnia in an epic battle as they confront Miraz.

Jack finished the book by Christmas 1949, and he quickly sent it off to his publisher. While Jack started on another story, Geoffrey wrote back and suggested that the book be published under the title *Prince Caspian* rather than the original *Drawn into Narnia.* Jack agreed to the change, with the proviso that it also have the subtitle *The Return to Narnia.*

With the second book in his series of stories about Narnia completed, Jack threw a luncheon for his friends where he read selections from the manuscript to them and introduced them to Pauline Baynes. Pauline was an artist whose illustrations in Tolkien's book *Farmer Giles of Ham* had impressed Jack. Much to his delight, Jack's publisher had agreed that Pauline could do the illustrations for *The Lion, the Witch and the Wardrobe,* and he hoped, for the second book as well.

The third book in the series that Jack embarked upon was titled *The Voyage of the* Dawn Treader. The story opens with Lucy and Edmund Pevensie standing with their obnoxious cousin, Eustace Clarence Scrubb, staring at a wall that held a picture of an ancient sailing ship. As they stare, the picture seems to come alive, and the three children are pulled into it. The children soon find themselves splashing about in the ocean and are rescued by the crew of the *Dawn Treader,* the ship in the picture. The ship is under the command of Lord Drinian, and aboard the vessel is Prince Caspian. The prince explains that he is on a quest to find seven of his father's friends, Lord Revilian, Lord Bern, Lord Argoz, Lord Mavramorn, Lord Octesian, Lord Restimar, and Lord Rhoop, all of whom had been deposed by Miraz. The men had vanished in the Eastern Seas beyond the Lone Islands at the outer limits of Narnia. The only problem is, no one aboard the *Dawn Treader* has ever voyaged into these waters before, and they have no idea what might lie ahead. Along the way many adventures ensue, the circumstances of which slowly transform Eustace Scrubb physically and spiritually. Aslan also shows up in the story and reveals many truths about the eternal world he inhabits.

By March 1950, *The Voyage of the* Dawn Treader was complete. Jack now had three books in various stages of publication. *The Lion, the Witch and the Wardrobe* was in the process of being typeset and illustrated, *Prince Caspian* was being proofread, and Jack was reading *The Voyage of the* Dawn Treader to Roger Green and listening carefully to his friend's feedback.

Jack also started work on the fourth book in the series, *The Wild Waste Lands,* which eventually became *The Silver Chair.* This story involved the much-changed Eustace Clarence Scrubb and Jill Pole, who both attend a school called Experiment House, where bullies mercilessly pick on them. One day Eustace tells Jill about Narnia, and moments later they find themselves standing on a precipice there. Aslan has summoned them, and he admonishes the two children:

> Far from here in the land of Narnia there lives an aged king. He has no heir because his only son was stolen from him many years ago and no one in Narnia knows where that prince went or whether he is alive. But he is. I lay on you this command, that you seek this lost prince until either you have found him and brought him to his father's house, or else died in the attempt, or else gone back into your own world.

Jill and Eustace take up the challenge and head for the ruined city of the ancient giants. Along the way they link up with Puddleglum, a Marsh-wiggle from the Eastern Marshes of Narnia, and encounter the Green Witch before arriving at the House of Harfang, where one of the giants has a cookbook with a recipe that begins, "MAN. This elegant little biped has long been valued as a delicacy."

On more than one occasion Jill and Eustace lose sight of their mission, but eventually they overcome the odds against them, find Prince Rilian, the son of Prince Caspian the Tenth, cut him free from the silver chair where he has been bound, and fight their way back to Narnia with him. And when Jill and Eustace finally make it back to their world, they find that the strength and confidence they have gained as a result of their mission allows them to beat back the bullies who tormented them in the past.

In April 1950, as Jack was working at writing *The Silver Chair,* Mrs. Moore fell out of bed and injured herself. After attending to Janie's injury, Dr. Havard explained to Jack that she could no longer stay in the house at The Kilns. She needed around-the-clock supervision and would have to be admitted to a geriatric nursing home. Jack accepted the doctor's diagnosis and chose nearby Restholme, in North Oxford, to which Mrs. Moore was transported. It was not cheap for Janie to stay there, costing over five hundred pounds per year. Jack worried about how he would pay for her care if she lived much more than another year or two. He put his thoughts about placing Mrs. Moore in a rest home on paper in a letter to Arthur Greeves, informing him that because of the added financial burden he could not afford to visit Ireland later that year. "I hardly know how to feel. Relief, pity, hope, terror, and bewilderment have me in a whirl. I have the jitters!"

Both Warren and Jack found it difficult to adjust to life at The Kilns without Janie Moore around. Janie had had a dominating influence on Jack's life for over thirty years, and now she was neatly tucked in bed in a nursing home with other people to care for her. There was no more of her yelling down the stairs at The Kilns, no more ranting insults, no more irregular meals worked around her needs. All was calm and peaceful. And even though Jack visited Mrs. Moore every day without fail, he still had much more free time than he'd ever known as an adult.

Of course he put this spare time to good use finishing *The Silver Chair* and starting in on the next book, *The Horse and His Boy,* though Jack initially titled it *Journey into Narnia.* "This is the story," Jack points out in the opening paragraph to the book, "of an adventure that happened in Narnia and Calormen and the lands between, in the Golden Age when Peter was High King in Narnia and his brother and his two sisters were King and Queens under him."

Essentially the story involved Shasta, a northern boy found in an abandoned boat by a poor fisherman named Arsheesh and forced to be the fisherman's slave. When Shasta learns that Arsheesh is trying to sell him to a man named Anradin, he decides to escape. Bree, Anradin's horse, who happens to be a talking horse from Narnia who was caught and pressed into Anradin's service, aids Shasta in escaping. The two make their escape, and on the way north they join up with Aravis Tarkheena and her talking horse. Aravis is a determined young woman from Calormen who is fleeing from an arranged marriage to a sixty-year-old man.

In late fall 1950, *The Lion, the Witch and the Wardrobe* was finally published. It received mixed reviews from the critics, and at first sales were slow. But as more and more children read the book and told their friends about it, sales began to grow, much to Jack's delight, since he had written the story for children, after all. Each December for the next six years, a new book in the series of stories about Narnia was published. Although Jack didn't know it at the time, none of these books would ever go out of print.

While New Year 1951 should have been a happy time for Jack, with the recent publication of *The Lion, the Witch and the Wardrobe* and four more books in the series completed, it turned out to be one of the most wrenching times in his life. By the end of the first week of January, Mrs. Moore lay seriously ill in her bed at Restholme with the flu. A week later, on January 12, with Jack at her side, she died. Jack thought he was prepared for the swirl of emotions her death would bring, but he had not realized that her death would also make his own mother's death forty-three years before seem so fresh to him all over again.

Janie Moore was buried in the churchyard at Headington Quarry on a particularly cold Monday afternoon. Warren, who had caught the same strain of flu as Mrs. Moore had died of, was not able to attend, though he did write in his diary about her passing.

> And so ends the mysterious self imposed slavery in which J[ack] has lived for at least thirty years. . . . It is quite idle, but none the less fascinating to muse on what his life might have been if he had never had the crushing misfortune to meet her: when one thinks of what he has accomplished even under that immense handicap. . . . I don't think I ever saw J work more than half an hour without the cry of "Baw-boys"! [her pet name for Jack]—"COMING Dear"!, down would go the pen, and he would be away perhaps five minutes, perhaps half an hour: possibly to do nothing more important than stand by the kitchen range as scullery maid. Then another spell of work, then the same thing all over again: and these were the conditions under which *Screwtape,* and indeed all his books were produced. What I think limited J more even than this, was the impossibility of knowing to within an hour and a half, when any meal would be on the table; for his presence was always required in the kitchen throughout the preparation. I wonder how much of his time she did waste?

Obviously this was not the whole picture, and because Jack kept his private life completely to himself—even guarding against his brother's knowing what went on between him and Mrs. Moore—no one will ever know exactly what attracted Jack to her and what kept him so loyal to her till the end.

One of Warren's assumptions, though, is quite wrong. Somehow Jack's creative abilities thrived around Mrs. Moore. In fact, Jack was able to write twenty-five books while living at The Kilns with her. And Jack also had many fond memories of her, particularly in the early days. It was Janie Moore, and not his father, who had visited him before he went off to World War I. She was the one who wrote to him every day, encouraging him and giving him hope that he would survive. And when he returned to England a wounded soldier, she stayed beside him for five months, helping him to heal.

But now it was time for Jack to go on alone. He was a fifty-two-year-old, single, plump, red-faced man, who concluded that the useful part of his life was probably behind him. But despite this piece of gloomy self-assessment, more did lie ahead for Jack. For one thing he had two more of his Narnia stories to write, and just three weeks after Mrs. Moore's death, he had another possibility to explore—the Chair of Poetry at Oxford.

Jack decided to enter the election for the Chair, and he had only one rival in the contest—Cecil Day Lewis. Surprisingly, not only did the two men share the same last name, but also they had a lot of other things in common. Like Jack, Cecil was born in Ireland, at Ballintubber in Queen's County, where his father was a Protestant clergyman. Following the death of Cecil's mother when he was a boy, Cecil's father, with the help of an aunt, brought Cecil up in London. Cecil Day Lewis had graduated from Wadham College, Oxford, in 1927, and in Oxford he was part of the circle that gathered around poet W. H. Auden and helped him edit *Oxford Poetry 1927*. His own first collection of poems, *Beechen Virgil*, had been published in 1925.

The race to become the new Chair of Poetry at Oxford was spirited and well fought, but Cecil eventually won the contest by a vote of 194 to 173. However, no one could be sure how accurate this count was, since the two men were listed on the voting slip as Lewis C. D. and Lewis C. S., and many of the voters may well have confused the two men.

Jack bore the defeat with dignity. Compared to being free from the daily drudgery of living at The Kilns with Mrs. Moore, it seemed a small thing. In fact, Jack worried about how happy he was and put his thoughts down in a letter to Sister Penelope:

> I specially need your prayers because I am (like the pilgrim in Bunyan) traveling across "a plain called Ease." Everything without, and many things within, are marvelously well at present.

With the election for the Chair of Poetry behind him, Jack turned his attention again to Narnia. This time he felt it was time to take up the story of *Polly and Digory,* which he had abandoned well over a year before. This time the story flowed for him; there was none of the bogging down because a character didn't belong, which had plagued his first attempt at the story. Quickly the story of the first humans to visit Narnia came together. The first paragraph of the story read, "This is a story about something that happened long ago when your grandfather was a child. It is a very important story because it shows how all the comings and goings between our own world and the land of Narnia first began."

The main human characters of the story are Polly Plummer, Digory Kirke, and Digory's uncle Andrew Ketterly, an amateur magician. Polly and Digory are neighbors in a row house in London who find a tunnel in the attic that connects their two homes. In this tunnel they discover a room where Andrew carries out his secret magic experiments. Andrew has made two rings from dust contained in a box from Atlantis. The yellow ring will carry the wearer to what Digory's uncle calls the "Other Place," and the green ring will bring the wearer back to this world. Andrew tricks Polly into touching the yellow ring, and Polly is instantly transported to the Other Place. Digory's uncle then tricks Digory into going after Polly. Adventures await Polly and Digory in this strange place, and the two meet a woman named Jadis, whom Digory thinks is the most beautiful woman he has ever seen. Eventually Jadis follows the two children back to this world, where she wreaks havoc in London. In the process she pulls the crossbar from a lamppost and uses it to attack a policeman. Digory and Polly promptly transport Jadis and several other residents of London back to the Other Place, where they meet Aslan and watch as he sings a creation song that calls the land of Narnia into being.

Jack reveals to his readers that in Narnia, Jadis will become the White Witch of *The Lion, the Witch and the Wardrobe* and that the crossbar of the lamp-post she brings back will grow to become the lamp-post at the edge of Narnia that serves as a marker and guide for the Pevensie children to find the back of the wardrobe. He also reveals that Digory returns to our world carrying a magic apple, which he feeds to his dying mother, who is then miraculously healed. Digory then buries the apple core in the garden, and an apple tree grows. Years later when the tree is blown down, Digory uses its wood to build a wardrobe—a magical wardrobe that serves as a gateway to Narnia. Jack also informs his readers that Digory Kirke is indeed Professor Kirke, to whose house the Pevensie children are evacuated in *The Lion, the Witch and the Wardrobe.*

Satisfied with the story, Jack sent it off to his publisher. Geoffrey Bles wrote back suggesting that the name of the story be changed from *Polly and Digory* to *The Magician's Nephew.* Jack agreed.

It was now time for Jack to turn his attention to the final book in the series. Jack titled the book *Night Falls on Narnia* and set to work. He carefully crafted a set of circumstances that would lead to a final climactic battle in Narnia. When he sees what he is up against, King Tirian of Narnia calls out, "Children! Children! Friends of Narnia! Quick. Come to me. Across the worlds I call you." Jill Pole and Eustace Scrubb are transported to Narnia in response to the king's cry for help, as are Peter, Edmund, and Lucy Pevensie. As the book draws to a close, Aslan in all his glory makes his final appearance. Also, Jack reveals to his readers what has happened to long-forgotten creatures they have met in the earlier books.

With the final book written, Jack breathed a sigh of relief and sent it on to his publisher, who, as he had with several of the other books, suggested that the title be changed. The new title of this book would be *The Last Battle.*

Finally, what Jack referred to as his Narnian Chronicles were complete. In a period of about two years Jack had written the seven books that made up the series, though not all of them had yet been published. As Jack flipped back through the copies of the manuscripts he had written, he was surprised at just how much Christian theology had found its way into the stories. He hadn't set out to write a set of religious stories, but even he had to admit that the stories of Narnia seemed to give a better and clearer picture of his Christian beliefs than many of his theological books.

While Narnia would never completely leave Jack, it was time for him to move on to the next chapter in his life, though one more name change would occur before the books would become known as they are today. Although Jack had referred to the books as his

Narnian Chronicles, Geoffrey Bles was not happy with this as a title for the series. It was then that Roger Green suggested switching the name around and calling the stories The Chronicles of Narnia. That name resonated with the publisher, and that is what the series of books was named.

Now it really was time for Jack to move on.

Chapter 14

New Opportunities

By September 1952, two of The Chronicles of Narnia, *The Lion, the Witch and the Wardrobe* and *Prince Caspian,* were published, and Jack was eagerly awaiting the publication of *The Voyage of the* Dawn Treader in December. As a result of the publication of the Narnia stories, Jack began receiving more fan mail than ever. Together he and Warren tried to answer each letter, but it was a daunting task. Many of the letters contained deeply personal questions about faith, marriage, and struggles with bad habits like drinking too much. Jack and Warren did their best to answer each person's questions as frankly and honestly as they could. From time to time, when Jack thought it would be helpful to a person, he would arrange to meet face to face with the person and attempt to resolve his or her problems.

One person he particularly enjoyed corresponding with was an American woman named Joy Gresham. Joy had first written to him in January 1950, telling him that she was a thirty-six-year-old mother from Westchester, New York, stuck in a very unhappy marriage. She had been born into a nonpracticing Jewish home and had become an atheist and then a communist. Then, as her marriage began to unravel, she had turned to Jesus Christ. At first her husband had been interested in Christianity too, and the pair had even written articles for Christian magazines. But Joy's husband's interest in religion died as Joy's grew stronger. And it was about her faith that Joy was interested in corresponding with Jack.

Jack was particularly struck with the intelligent questions Joy asked and the way that she doggedly pursued her own writing career. Joy had a master of arts degree from Columbia University and had won a prize in poetry writing, and at the time she was writing a book on the Ten Commandments. While Jack enjoyed his lively correspondence with her, he was still surprised when she wrote to say that she was leaving the United States and coming to England for an extended visit. She asked if she could meet Jack, and he set up a luncheon date for them to get together at Magdalen College.

Before Joy arrived in Oxford, though, Jack enjoyed a wonderful holiday visiting ruined castles in North Wales. Roger Green accompanied Jack on the trip, and the two of them hatched a plan to spice up their vacation. They booked their rooms separately at the Bulkeley Arms at Beaumaris on Anglesey. They arrived at the inn separately and checked into their rooms, keeping up the pretense that the one man did not know the other. Later, in the dining room, they both put on quite a show, pretending to meet by chance and striking up a conversation.

The following day Jack and Roger visited the ruins of a nearby castle, and Jack was greatly impressed by them. As the two men sat atop the castle's old tower, they began hatching the plot of a story together. They pretended that they were the only survivors of a worldwide cataclysm and then later discovered a group of children who had also survived. Together they all decide to found a new civilization.

As they hatched their plot, Jack and Roger paid close attention to what important facts of religion, literature, history, science, and general knowledge they could call to mind to be handed on to the children who would be the founders and keepers of the new civilization. It was a creative and intellectual exercise that seemed to stimulate both men, who were still devising what knowledge they would pass on when they visited Conway Castle the next day.

Jack arrived back in Oxford feeling refreshed and invigorated from his vacation with Roger. On his return he found two interesting pieces of mail waiting for him at home. One was a brand-new copy of *The Voyage of the* Dawn Treader, the third book in The Chronicles of Narnia series. The other was a letter from Joy Gresham. Joy had arrived in London and was looking forward to meeting Jack soon. Jack grew nervous as he prepared to meet this woman with whom he had shared a personal correspondence for two years.

Finally the day of their meeting arrived. Joy took a train from London to Oxford, where she had booked into the Eastgate Hotel, directly across the road from Magdalen College, where Jack and Warren met her for lunch. Joy was an attractive woman of medium height, with dark hair and sharp features. She was vivacious and every bit the brash, intellectual American woman that Jack had imagined her to be. She peppered the stories she told with slang and seemed to have no idea what was a proper "English" line of conversation in a mixed group. Warren and others were taken aback by her manner of speaking, but Jack found it refreshing and direct. He spent much of their lunch laughing at the shocking observations she made about English culture.

When Joy returned to London, Jack found himself missing her, and so he invited her to The Kilns for Christmas. It was supposed to be a short visit, but she ended up staying for two weeks. During this time the two of them took long walks in the country and visited some of Jack's favorite places. Jack read the manuscript Joy was working on and offered some advice for strengthening it, and Joy, in turn, read some of Jack's unpublished writing.

During this time together over Christmas, Joy confided in Jack the full extent of her marital problems. Her husband, Bill Gresham, was a well-known novelist in the United States. In fact, his first novel,

Nightmare Alley, had been turned into a movie in 1947, netting him the sum of sixty thousand dollars. However, he had gone through the money on alcohol, bad living, and ensuing tax problems. Fortunately, Joy's cousin Renée Pierce had agreed to come from Florida to New York to stay with Bill and look after their two boys while Joy traveled to England.

On her final day at The Kilns, Joy received a letter from her husband. As she read it she became distraught. "Renée and I are in love and have been since the middle of August," Bill Gresham wrote. Then he asked for a divorce, outlining the long-term arrangement he preferred. Joy could get remarried "to some really swell guy, Renée and I to be married, both families to live in easy calling distance so that the Gresham kids could have a Mommy and Daddy on hand."

Joy went straight to Jack with the letter and poured out her heart to him. Jack was shocked that any man, especially a man who had called himself a Christian, could be that callous and calculating. Joy indicated that she would do her best to try to fix the situation when she got back home to the United States.

By the summer of 1953, it was obvious that Joy's marriage was over. In the divorce settlement Joy received custody of her two sons and monetary support from Bill, though she seriously doubted that she would see much of that. Bill was now free to marry Joy's cousin Renée, but Joy had no intention of completing the cozy living arrangement by moving a block or two away. Instead, she sold her belongings and set sail for England, this time with her two young sons, David and Douglas, in tow. She found a hotel in Belsize Park, London, in which to stay and immediately enrolled the boys at an expensive private school, Dane Court, in Surrey.

When Jack learned of Joy's return to England, he took financial responsibility for her sons' education, just as he had done for Maureen when he met Mrs. Moore. The money for their education was to be paid through the charity Jack had set up, using income from the royalties on his books.

Jack saw little of Joy after her return to England, since he was not interested in traveling to London and she was busy writing. But he did invite her and the boys to The Kilns for four days in December. Jack found David Gresham to be a little withdrawn and sullen, while his younger brother Douglas seemed to be a much happier, more adaptable boy.

When seven-year-old Douglas laid eyes on the large wardrobe parked in the corner of the hallway at The Kilns, he asked, "Is that *the* wardrobe?"

"It might be!" Jack replied.

Douglas was entranced by the magic wardrobe he had read about in *The Lion, the Witch and the Wardrobe,* but he also kept his distance from it, not yet ready to open it and step inside for fear of where it might transport him.

Of the visit, Jack wrote in a letter, "Last week we entertained a lady from New York for four days, with her boys aged nine and seven respectively. . . . It however went swimmingly, though it was very, very exhausting. The energy of the modern American boy is astonishing; this pair thought nothing of a four mile hike across broken country as an incident in a day of ceaseless activity, and when we took them up Magdalen tower, they said as soon as we got back to ground, 'Let's do it again.'"

Before David and Douglas Gresham left The Kilns with their mother to return to London, Jack gave them each a typewritten copy of *The Horse and His Boy* and told them that he was going to dedicate the published version of the book to them.

Jack and Joy saw a little more of each other after the December visit, but both of them were also very busy in their own spheres. Joy had been spurred on to finish writing *Smoke on the Mountain,* her book on the Ten Commandments, by Jack's willingness to write a foreword for it. The fact that it would have the name C. S. Lewis on the cover made the book a much easier pitch to a publisher, and Joy intended to take full advantage of the offer. Meanwhile, Jack was exploring a new career possibility.

The idea of leaving a college where you had lectured for twenty-nine years would have been a wrenching experience for most people, but for Jack it was particularly painful, since he hated any kind of change. But the opportunity had come out of the blue, and Jack felt he had to investigate it. In 1954, Magdalene College in Cambridge established a new professorship, or "Chair," concentrating on medieval and Renaissance literature. Many of Jack's colleagues and friends urged him to apply for the position, but

Jack felt stuck. According to the terms that Jack and Warren had agreed to when they bought The Kilns, the place did not belong to either of them. Instead, the brothers got to live there for as long as they wanted, but when they died—or left—The Kilns became the property of Maureen Moore.

Jack did not think he could afford to buy a new place in which to live in Cambridge, nor did he think that Warren would be happy with such a change. His only glimmer of hope that Warren might be all right without him was the fact that Warren was having some modest success in his own writing career. Warren had always been fascinated with French history and had been writing a book titled *The Splendid Century: Some Aspects of French Life in the Reign of Louis XIV.* He had just completed the book and found a publisher for it, and now he was eager to begin a sequel titled *The Sunset of the Splendid Century: The Life and Times of Louis Auguste de Bourbon, Duc de Maine, 1670–1736.*

Yet, as he weighed his options, Jack realized that he had burned many bridges at Magdalen College, Oxford, and as a result he would never get a promotion there. Much of the problem revolved around his prominent position as a Christian writer. Many of his colleagues felt that he had "lowered the tone" of the English department at Magdalen College by writing for common people and then, even more scandalously, for children. This, along with Jack's weariness at tutoring an endless stream of undergraduates, had made him the target of many veiled complaints.

Eventually Jack decided that he was better suited to the professorship at Cambridge, though he loathed the idea of moving all his books there, making new friends, and adjusting to a new set of college politics. Thankfully, though, the decision to make the transition was made easier for him when his Cambridge supporters suggested that he continue to live at The Kilns at Oxford and spend term days from Monday afternoon to Friday afternoon at Cambridge. Jack felt that he could live with this arrangement, and he put in his resignation at Magdalen College, Oxford, and accepted the new post at Magdalene College, Cambridge.

Jack's inauguration in his new position as professor came before he officially moved into his new rooms at the college. It was one of the most memorable inaugurations of Jack's life. The event occurred on November 29, 1954, Jack's fifty-sixth birthday. When he arrived at the hall to give his inauguration speech, the place was completely packed. There were so many people, in fact, that the group of friends, colleagues, and old students from Oxford who had traveled to Cambridge for the event could find nowhere to sit. Eventually they were accommodated on the stage behind Jack.

Once the introduction and other formalities were dispensed with, Jack pulled his gown around him and stood to address the gathered crowd. The subject of his lecture was his assertion that a great divide in culture had taken place between the time of Jane Austen and the present day. In a spirited delivery

Jack gave examples of how changes in politics, art, religion, and, in particular, modern technology had altered man's place in nature. As a result mankind had embraced a new myth—that the new is better. Jack pointed out that he was not a part of this new order. He was a "dinosaur"—a part of the old order. He then encouraged his listeners to draw on the combined knowledge of men like him so that they could broaden their cultural understanding by embracing the old order.

Once Jack had spoken, the audience erupted into applause, and such comments as "We were overwhelmed by his vitality and enthusiasm" and "I have never heard a lecture anywhere near as exciting" were heard around the hall. For weeks afterward it was not uncommon to hear students at Cambridge referring to themselves as "dinos."

Jack's official duties at Cambridge as Professor C. S. Lewis began in January 1955, and Joy came to Oxford to help him pack up his office. It was a bittersweet time for Jack as he recalled the many years he had spent in those rooms. He thought of the secret trips to visit Mrs. Moore during his early years as a student, the evenings spent discussing manuscripts with J. R. R. Tolkien and Hugo Dyson, and the sound of Warren tapping away at the typewriter as he produced the Lewis family history. Now, as he approached old age, Jack was about to embark upon a new adventure—even if it was reluctantly.

Chapter 15

The Two Weddings of C. S. Lewis

"I am tall, fat, bald, red-faced, double-chinned, black-haired and wear glasses for reading," Jack wrote in response to a letter from a schoolgirl in the United States who wanted to know what he looked like. His description was accurate, though it did not carry any hint of his enthusiasm for life and his lively imagination—traits that had to be discovered in person.

After initially dreading the move to Magdalene College, Cambridge, Jack quickly embraced the change, calling it a great adventure. He was glad to be done with tutoring a never-ending flow of undergraduates and able to concentrate more on lectures and writing. His life soon fell into a routine that allowed him the time and energy to do this.

The new rooms Jack was assigned at Magdalene College were smaller and not as well appointed or comfortable as his rooms in Oxford, but Jack took this in stride. There were lots of other things to like about Cambridge. The town was smaller and quieter than Oxford, and Magdalene College offered a more relaxed atmosphere in which to work. Also, the college's fellows were much more friendly and courteous than those at Magdalen had been. Jack also liked the leisurely train trip from Oxford to Cambridge and back each week. The train was usually almost empty, affording him plenty of time to read and think.

Once he had arrived at Cambridge, Jack settled into his weekly routine. He would rise early each morning and attend chapel service, after which he would eat breakfast and then retire to his rooms to go over his correspondence. The flow of fan letters was ceaseless, and with Warren back at The Kilns in Oxford, Jack was left to respond to most of the letters on his own. (Jack had employed Mrs. Miller to come to The Kilns from Tuesday through Friday to cook for and generally look after Warren.) After going over his correspondence, Jack would then prepare or give lectures until lunchtime. Following lunch he would take a long walk through the surrounding countryside, followed by a cup of tea, and then he would spend the rest of the afternoon and evening reading and writing.

Now that he was a professor at Cambridge, Jack's income had tripled, easing the financial situation at home. In addition, royalties from his books continued to flow in (though they also flowed out through Jack's charitable trust).

Soon after Jack made his move to Magdalene College, Joy Gresham made a move of her own. She had just secured a publisher for her book *Smoke on the Mountain: An Interpretation of the Ten Commandments,* which she had decided to publish under her maiden name, Joy Davidman. She had dedicated the book to Jack, and in turn he had written a flattering foreword for it. With the book behind her, Joy had decided to move to Oxford to be nearer to Jack. At first Jack was not sure about this move. He described Joy in a letter as "our queer, Jewish, ex-communist, American convert." Nonetheless he had a soft spot for her and not only found her a place to live a mile from The Kilns but also signed up to pay the rent on the place.

This move brought about some interesting outcomes for both Jack and Joy. Jack had just finished writing an autobiographical book called *Surprised by Joy: The Shape of My Early Life.* Of course the *joy* he was talking about was not Joy Gresham but the overpowering feeling that he had sensed when he embraced Christianity. The book dealt mainly with his childhood—the loss of his mother, the terror of boarding school, and his Christian conversion—though it left out some of the most interesting parts of his story. For instance, Jack did not mention his thirty-year relationship with Mrs. Moore, nor did he acknowledge that his father's death had any effect on him at all. But with *Surprised by Joy* now at the publishers, for the first time in many years, perhaps ever, Jack could not think of a single thing he wanted to write. His mind was blank.

On one of his visits to Joy's house in April 1955, Jack confided his predicament to her. Joy poured them both something to drink, and they began discussing ideas for book topics. Before the end of the evening, they had settled on *Bareface.* The story revolved around the retelling of the ancient myth of Cupid and Psyche, which Jack had first encountered while a student at Malvern College. In telling the story, Jack would try a different approach. Unlike his other works of fiction, which had all been written in the third person, Jack would write this book in the first person, telling the story from the point of view of Orual, queen of Glome and the sister of Psyche.

As the project progressed, Jack and Joy found that they worked well together. This was a surprise, since both of them were very independent writers who had never collaborated before. They began each chapter by discussing what it should contain, and then Jack would write the chapter in longhand. Joy would then edit what he had written and type it out. They would then read over each completed chapter together and make any changes necessary before moving on to write the next chapter. Working in this manner they made fast progress, and the book was finished and ready for typesetting by February 1956. The only thing they did not have for the book by then was a title that satisfied Jack's publisher, Geoffrey Bles.

Although Jack and Joy both liked the title *Bareface,* Geoffrey did not, telling Jack that the book might be mistaken for a western. Jack did not agree. He thought that *Bareface* captured the thrust of the book's story better than any other title. However, Jack also trusted his publisher's judgment, and eventually he came up with the title *Till We Have Faces*. Geoffrey accepted the new title.

In December 1955, *The Magician's Nephew* was published in time for the Christmas market. This was the sixth year in a row that a new book in The Chronicles of Narnia series was published, and the book soon climbed the Christmas bestseller list, much to the delight of Jack and thousands of his young fans. However, when *Till We Have Faces* was finally published in September 1956, it did not make such a big impression on the public. Jack was disappointed with the slow sales in England, though it did sell better in the United States. Yet, while sales were slow, the book did garner some positive reviews.

According to the *Times Literary Supplement, Till We Have Faces* was a profound allegory. The *New York Times Book Review* stated that in the book "love is quite literally given wings again." And Anthony Boucher, an American reviewer, declared *Till We Have Faces* to be "a masterwork," Jack's "major work to date." He then went on to declare, "As a story, as a fantasy, as a study in human psychology, as a grappling with spiritual dilemmas, above all as a work of art this book is magic."

In the spring of 1956, Joy had approached Jack with a problem—and a solution. She and her two sons, now ages eleven and twelve, had been staying in England on visitors' visas. The visas were about to run out, and the British government had decided not to allow the Greshams to renew them. Because Joy had always assumed that she would spend the rest of her life in England, the pending expiration of their visas came as a shocking blow. Joy was now faced with uprooting her boys and returning to the United States, unless she became a British citizen. And the only way to do that, she told Jack, was to marry an Englishman, and the Englishman she had set her sights on was Jack.

Jack viewed the idea as a business deal. Joy needed a piece of paper that said she was married to an Englishman, and Jack was in a position to be able to help her get that piece of paper. It would be a strictly civil matter, nothing to do with really being man and wife before God, and nothing else about their relationship would change. Jack's friend George Sayer disagreed with this assessment and strongly tried to talk Jack out of going through with it. He asked what would happen if Joy died. Jack replied that he was ready to take legal responsibility for the boys in that circumstance. And what if Joy fell in love with someone and wanted to marry the person? She would have to divorce Jack first in order to do so, and then Jack would be a divorced man. These were all valid objections, but for whatever reason, Jack chose to dismiss them. On April 23, 1956, Joy Gresham and C. S. Lewis were married in a civil ceremony held at the Oxford Registry Office. Warren knew of the arrangement, but most other people did not, including Maureen Moore and J. R. R. Tolkien.

Subtle changes began to occur in Jack's life after the civil service. He took more of an interest in his "stepsons." He taught David Latin and bought a pony for Douglas to ride when the family came to visit The Kilns. He also began visiting Joy late each night when he was in Oxford and found himself spending less and less time with Warren. In fact, Jack was spending so much time with Joy that she began hinting that now that they were legally married, it would be much easier for everyone if she and the boys moved into The Kilns.

Meanwhile, things were going well in Jack's new position at Cambridge, so well, in fact, that in October 1956 he was asked to consider becoming chairman of the Faculty Board of English at Cambridge. By now Jack was quite aware of his own limitations and had no need to prove himself to others. He replied to the offer in a letter:

> No. It would never do. People so often deny their own capacity for business either through mock-modesty or through laziness that when the denial happens to be true, it is difficult to make it convincing. But I have been tried at this kind of job; and none of those who experienced me in office ever wanted to repeat the experience. I am both muddlesome and forgetful. Quite objectively, I'd be a disaster. But thank you for your suggestion.

It was a good thing that Jack turned down the position, because within days his and Joy's lives were turned upside down.

It was October 18, 1956, a cold, dreary fall day. Joy was sitting in a chair in her house at Headington Quarry when the telephone rang. She got up to answer the phone, and in the process she tripped on the phone cord. As she tumbled to the floor, she felt the femur in her left leg snap. Despite the searing pain, Joy kept her wits about her, reached for the telephone receiver, and told the person on the other end of the line, Katherine Farrer, wife of the local Anglican vicar, her predicament. Katherine quickly hung up and called for an ambulance, and Joy was soon transported to the hospital.

Over the previous few months Joy had been experiencing pain in her upper leg, back, and chest that sometimes made it difficult for her to walk. The condition had been diagnosed as fibrositis, but X-rays taken at the hospital after her accident showed this diagnosis to be wrong. Joy's condition was much worse. She had a cancerous tumor in her left femur that had weakened the bone, causing it to snap when she fell. Worse still, her doctor discovered that she also had malignant tumors in her right leg, one of her shoulders, and her left breast. The doctor explained that the tumor in the breast was most likely the primary site for the cancer and it had spread from there into her bones.

This was devastating news. Joy was only forty-two years old, and her prospects for living a long life were now almost zero. According to her doctor, perhaps she would live for a few more months, or maybe even a year. In the meantime, immediate steps were taken to try to stop the spread of the cancer. In the course of three operations over the following month, the tumor growth in her femur was removed and the bone repaired, the tumor in her breast was removed, and her ovaries were taken out.

Jack, of course, spent many hours at Joy's hospital bedside. The more time he spent with her, the more he felt his feelings toward her intensifying. It became obvious to him that he had fallen in love with Joy, and she with him. This situation presented a strange quandary; they were already married in the eyes of the law, and now they wanted to be married in the eyes of God. But Jack was a staunch defender of the Anglican Church and one of its leading lay authors and public speakers, and the church forbade divorced people from remarrying. So what were he and Joy to do?

Jack thought about the dilemma and decided to talk to Harry Carpenter, the bishop of Oxford. He explained the situation to the bishop, who listened attentively. Harry was sympathetic to Jack's plight, but he explained that the Church of England could neither conduct nor condone such a marriage. Church doctrine forbade divorced people from remarrying. Jack responded by making the argument that since Bill Gresham had been married and divorced before he met Joy, the Gresham marriage had never been a proper marriage, since in the eyes of God (who according to church doctrine does not recognize divorce) Bill was still married to his first wife. Harry explained that in the Catholic Church such an argument could well be persuasive and lead to an annulment, allowing the parties to then marry, but not in the Anglican Church. Joy was a divorcee with two sons—that was all there was to it—and the Church of England could not condone Jack's marriage to her.

Jack went away from his meeting with the bishop feeling dejected and unsure of how to proceed. Several months passed as he struggled with what to do. At the same time Joy's health remained in a precarious position. Since Joy was much too ill to bring "home" to The Kilns, Jack and Warren took care of her boys, which wasn't an easy task.

Thankfully, Maureen, who had just learned of Jack's secret civil marriage to Joy, arrived at The Kilns in early January 1957 and took the two boys back with her to Malvern, where she lived with her husband and their two young children. The arrangement was only temporary, but the idea was that if they all got along well together, Maureen and her husband might keep the boys once Joy died. Unfortunately, they did not all get along. Maureen found David a very difficult child to handle. She was sure he stole money from her and bullied her young daughter. As a result, the boys were soon back at The Kilns, with their "legal" stepfather—Jack.

In the midst of all that was going on in Jack's life, the seventh and final book in The Chronicles of Narnia, *The Last Battle,* was published in December 1956. Jack hardly had time to notice.

As Jack continued to watch Joy suffer, the name Peter Bide came to his mind. Peter had been a student at Oxford studying English literature. He was an older student, having started out as a chemist before deciding he enjoyed literature more. While he was not one of Jack's students, he had attended a number of Jack's lectures. Peter, Jack learned, was now an ordained Anglican vicar with a gift of healing.

Jack wrote to Peter and asked him to come to Oxford and pray for Joy's healing. Peter soon arrived in Oxford, and with Jack at his side, he went to the hospital, where he laid his hands on Joy's head and prayed that God would heal her.

After Peter had prayed for Joy, he and Jack talked together about the predicament Jack and Joy found themselves in. Jack repeated his argument that Bill Gresham had been married and divorced before he married Joy, and therefore, in the eyes of God, Joy was never really married to Bill and was now free to marry Jack. He pointed out that for the Church of England to deny this point was to want to have it both ways, that Bill's marriage to Joy was and was not a Christian marriage. Like the bishop of Oxford, Peter listened attentively to all that Jack had to say. But unlike the bishop, he agreed with Jack's argument and could see no reason why Jack and Joy could not be married. He offered to conduct the service himself the following day. Jack breathed a sigh of relief, and a wedding was quickly arranged.

At eleven in the morning on March 21, 1957, Warren accompanied Jack to Joy's room at the hospital, where the Reverend Peter Bide was waiting for them. One of the ward nurses joined the group in Joy's room to act as a witness along with Warren. Peter married Jack and Joy in a religious service, after which he said mass and administered communion to the five people packed into the room. As far as Jack was concerned, he was now married to Joy both legally and, more important, spiritually.

The following morning the *Times* carried an announcement of the wedding. "A marriage has taken place between Professor C. S. Lewis of Magdalene College, Cambridge, and Mrs. Joy Gresham, now a patient in the Churchill Hospital at Oxford. It is requested that no letters be sent." Many of Jack's closest friends were dumbfounded when they read the announcement. Jack, as he had done with Janie Moore years before, had kept the nature of his relationship with Joy so secret that they had no idea he was even contemplating marriage to her.

In the course of a year, C. S. Lewis's whole life had been turned upside down. He was now married to a terminally ill woman and had her two sons to take care of. As well, the new school term had just begun, and Jack wondered how he would cope with what lay ahead.

Chapter 16

Some of the Happiest Days of His Life

Shortly after their marriage service, Joy was released from the hospital and went to live at The Kilns. Once there she began to feel better, amazing many people who had expected her to die soon after her discharge from the hospital. But Jack was not surprised. He saw the improvement in her health as the answer to a peculiar prayer he had prayed. In Oxford during the war Charles Williams had told him about a theory called "substitution," by which God would allow one person to bear another's pain. Jack had prayed and asked God to take Joy's pain away and give it to him instead. As Joy improved, Jack began to get sick. His condition was diagnosed as osteoporosis, a bone disease caused by lack of calcium. Sometimes Jack was in so much pain that he had to take strong medication to sleep, and Dr. Havard fitted him with a surgical back brace. Nonetheless, Jack was glad to shoulder the pain, since he believed that in doing so he was helping Joy to feel better. Now they faced ill health together.

Another matter the couple had to face together was the fate of David and Douglas if and when Joy died. The need to resolve this became apparent when the boys' father, Bill Gresham, wrote to Joy saying that he was sorry to hear of her illness, but in the event that she died, he would obviously want to regain custody of the boys. At hearing this, Jack swung into action, writing perhaps the most forceful letter he had ever written in his life. He told Bill that the boys belonged with him in England and that neither of them wanted to return to the United States and live with their father. In the course of the letter, Jack included a threat:

> If you do not relent, I shall of course be obliged to place every legal obstacle in your way. Joy has, legally, a case. Her (documented) desire for naturalization (which there may still be time to carry out) and the boys' horror of going back, will be strong points. What is certain is that a good deal of your money and mine will go into the lawyers' hands. You have a chance to soothe, instead of aggravating, the miseries of a woman you once loved. You have a chance of recovering at some future date, instead of alienating forever, the love and respect of your

children. For God's sake take it and yield to the deep wishes of everyone concerned except yourself.

Jack's stern letter seemed to settle the matter. Bill wrote back to say that he would not pursue custody of David and Douglas if and when Joy died. Instead, as their legal stepfather, Jack would assume custody of the two boys.

Both Jack and Joy were relieved to have the matter of the boys' custody behind them. They had another reason to be happy as well. Neither of them was experiencing pain. In fact, they both felt in great health. By December 1957 Joy was up and about and could walk a mile and do some gardening. It was a turn for the best that astonished those who watched, and which Jack called a miracle.

Jack felt so energized that he began work on a new project. During 1957 he had been approached by the Episcopal Radio-TV Foundation in Atlanta, Georgia, to write and record a series of talks for broadcast on the radio in the United States. After some negotiation, Jack agreed to do this, but he did not really get under way on the project until the start of 1958. The topic he decided on for the series was "The Four Loves," examining the four types of love mentioned in the New Testament. These four types of love in the Greek were *storge, philia, eros,* and *agape.* Writing the talks proved harder than Jack had first imagined, but by summer he had finished them, and on August 19 he traveled to London for two days to record them.

The tapes of the recording sessions were then shipped off to the United States for broadcast. The plan was to give the talks a wide airing on American radio stations, and a promotional campaign to drum up interest was begun. As it turned out, though, Jack's talks were never played widely on the radio in the United States. As part of his negotiation to write the series in the first place, however, Jack would be free to do with the radio script as he pleased after the talks were recorded. He decided to turn the script into a book. Making some revisions as he went, he completed the manuscript for *The Four Loves* by summer 1959, and the book was published in March 1960.

At the same time as he was preparing *The Four Loves* in 1958, Jack completed work on a book titled *Reflections on the Psalms,* the idea for which had come to him ten years before.

In July 1958, after finishing writing the script for *The Four Loves* and before going to London to record it, Jack and Joy flew together to Ireland. This was the first airplane ride either of them had ever taken. They were both nervous, and their knuckles were white from gripping the arms of their seats as the aircraft rumbled down the runway for takeoff. But once they were finally in the air, Jack and Joy relaxed and marveled at the beauty of the cloudscape laid out beneath them. The couple spent two weeks in Ireland and enjoyed every moment of the time together. When they returned to England, Jack wrote to a friend about the vacation. "We had a holiday—you might call it a belated honeymoon—in Ireland and were lucky enough to get that perfect fortnight in July. We visited Louth, Down, and Donegal, and returned drunk with blue mountains, yellow beaches, dark fuchsia, breaking waves, braying donkeys, peat-smell, and the heather just beginning to bloom."

The year 1959 began on an optimistic note for Jack and Joy. Jack had an article about Joy's health published in the *Atlantic Monthly* magazine, in which he declared,

> I have stood by the bedside of a woman whose thigh-bone was eaten through with cancer and who had thriving colonies of the disease in many other bones as well. It took three people to move her in bed. The doctors predicted a few months of life: the nurses (who often know better) a few weeks. A good man laid his hands on her and prayed. A year later the patient was walking (uphill, too, through the woodland) and the man who took the last X-ray photographs was saying "These bones are as solid as rock." It's miraculous.

During the weeks Jack continued his routine of going to Cambridge on Monday afternoons and returning to The Kilns and his wife on Friday afternoons. He savored the weekends when he would sit and talk with Joy and they would take long walks together.

This hiatus in Joy's cancer lasted for ten more months, when Jack took Joy back to the hospital to have what they thought would be her final cancer checkup. They both were expecting that she would be given a clean bill of health. Instead, they were blind-sided by devastating news: Joy's cancer, which had been in remission, had returned with a vengeance. "We are in retreat," Jack wrote afterward. "The tide has turned."

Indeed, the tide had turned. In the weeks that followed, Joy was often bedridden and again in terrible pain, but she was not yet willing to give in. As part of this determination not to give in, Jack and Joy booked a trip to Greece with Roger Green and his wife, June. As the departure date of Sunday, April 3, 1960, approached, despite her continued pain, Joy was more determined than ever to embark on this final adventure.

The two couples flew to Athens from London, the plane making two stops along the way to refuel. The following day Jack and Joy climbed the Acropolis, where they sat and took in the wonder and beauty of the Parthenon. They also made a day trip to Mycenae, where Jack was awestruck by the ruins, and another day trip to the Gulf of Corinth, before flying on to the island of Rhodes, which Jack categorized as an "earthly paradise." On Rhodes they attended Easter service at a Greek Orthodox cathedral. Jack was so impressed by the service and the atmosphere of the place that he declared that he preferred the Greek Orthodox liturgy to the liturgy of both the Roman Catholic Church and the Church of England.

From Rhodes they traveled on to Crete, where again they enjoyed exploring the local history and culture. As they traveled, their evenings were filled with long, relaxed dinners, during which they sampled all of the local delicacies.

Finally, after eleven days away, on April 14, Jack and Joy arrived back in London where a car was waiting to drive them back to The Kilns. As they were being driven to Oxford, Jack marveled at how Joy had handled herself on the trip. Despite her obvious pain, she never let it intrude on the enjoyment of others and, given her circumstance, was willing to give most things a go. Indeed, Jack decided that he had just passed some of the happiest days of his life, and he was elated that the two of them had managed to defy the odds and enjoy one last trip together.

But the exertion of the trip had taken its toll on Joy's health, and she never fully recovered her vitality. For the next three months Joy was in and out of the hospital for treatment for her cancer. She had one breast removed, but after that she refused any further surgery.

Despite the best efforts of the doctors at the hospital, by July 13, 1960, it was evident that the end for Joy was near. Jack had David and Douglas called home from boarding school, and then he stood vigil at his wife's bedside. "If you can, if it is allowed," he told Joy quietly, "come to me when I too am on my deathbed."

Joy smiled. "Allowed! Heaven would have a job to hold me; and as for Hell, I'd break it into bits," she replied, after which she asked Jack not to spend money on an expensive coffin for her and to have her body cremated. With those matters out of the way, she said, "I am at peace with God." These were the last words that Joy Lewis ever spoke.

Joy's funeral service was held on July 18, 1960. Jack had always kept his private life very separate from his public life, and perhaps as a result of this, only a handful of people came to pay their last respects.

Following the service Jack returned to The Kilns a lonely, heartbroken widower. He didn't know what to do with himself, so he did the only thing he knew how to do. He picked up a pen and started to write—this time about his grief.

Chapter 17

In the Shadowlands

Jack poured out his feelings onto the page in what would become the book titled *A Grief Observed*. In the deeply personal book, Jack described his feelings following Joy's death. He noted that through observing and seeking to understand the grief he was feeling, he was better able to control it. He also noted that in enduring such a deep and intense grief he had recovered the true essence of Joy. While she had passed on physically, Joy was now more alive within him than she had been in life.

When he was finished writing, Jack did not know what to do with the manuscript he had created. On the one hand the writing was so intensely honest that he felt sure it would help others come to terms with their own grief, but *because* it was so honest he did not want anyone to know he had written it. It would be too embarrassing for him to bare his soul so publicly, and he cringed at the type of personal "fan mail" such a book might generate. In the end, he arranged to have the book published under the pseudonym N. W. Clerk and swore his publisher to secrecy to protect his identity.

Because *A Grief Observed* did not have the name C. S. Lewis on its cover, the book did not sell well. Still, Jack didn't care. Writing the book had given him the courage to face life again. Even so, Jack had to admit that Joy's death, and the memories it recalled of his mother's death so long ago, had permanently changed him. He felt old and tired. Instead of taking the train to Cambridge, he now often took a taxi, and he no longer looked forward to the weekends as he once had.

Within a year of Joy's death, Jack realized that he too was ill. His prostate was malfunctioning, putting stress on his kidneys and heart. Dr. Havard put him on a strict diet and instructed him to sleep sitting up in a chair and not to climb stairs or overexert himself in any way. When all of those measures did not bring relief, Jack started a round of blood transfusions, which he found very trying. He remarked in a letter, "I've just had a blood transfusion and am feeling very drowsy. Dracula must have led a horrid life."

Throughout this trying time, Jack kept writing. *The Four Loves*, published in March 1960, was selling well, and Jack watched in delight as subsequent editions of many of his other books rolled off the presses.

By the beginning of 1962 Jack felt much better, and he was able to return to his duties at Magdalene College, Cambridge, for the spring term. He also liked to go for long drives in the countryside with his friends and to reread many of the classic books that he had loved since he was a boy.

During this time Jack received a letter from a young man in the United States by the name of Walter Hooper. Walter wanted to visit Jack and interview him for a book in a series of books on English authors. Jack wrote back to him, "Certainly I shall be happy to see you when you visit England. But I feel very strongly that a man is ill advised to write a book on any living author. There is bound to be at least one person, and there are probably several, who inevitably know more about the subject than ordinary research will discover. Far better write about the unanswering dead."

In September Jack received some bad news. Bill Gresham, David and Douglas's father, had been diagnosed with cancer. Rather than suffer through the pain of a slow death, Bill had taken his own life. Now Jack's stepsons had neither of their natural parents left. They had only him, their ailing, aging stepfather. It was not the best arrangement for two teenage boys, but Jack determined to make the most of the situation. He made a new will, leaving most of his assets in a trust for the boys so that they could finish their education. The remainder of his assets were to be put into a trust for Warren to use for as long as he lived. The will also stipulated that when Warren died, Jack's literary estate should belong to David and Douglas Gresham.

Jack's health continued to improve throughout 1962 and on into 1963. Jack was able to keep up with his classes at Cambridge, as well as with his reading and meeting with his friends.

In early 1963, Walter Hooper, the young American who had written to Jack the year before, finally came to visit. Jack liked him right away. Walter was a bright and insightful young man, and the two men soon fell into conversation at The Kilns. After two hours of talking, Jack escorted Walter to the bus stop to catch the bus back into Oxford, stopping along the way for a drink at Jack's favorite local pub, the Ampleforth Arms. Before Walter boarded the bus, Jack asked him to come back and visit him on Monday.

At their next meeting Jack gave Walter a copy of his latest manuscript, *Letters to Malcolm, Chiefly on Prayer.* Walter read the manuscript and discussed it with Jack on their third meeting. Soon Jack and Walter were meeting regularly three times a week. Jack found the meetings stimulating and Walter to be very helpful, so helpful, in fact, that in July Jack asked him to be his private secretary at The Kilns. Walter agreed, though he would have to return to the United States in September to take care of some pressing obligations, but as soon as he had, he would come straight back to Oxford.

In July 1963, Jack became ill again and was once more admitted to the hospital, where he suffered a mild heart attack. It was obvious to Jack that his teaching days were over, and he tendered his resignation from Magdalene College. The journey to and from Cambridge was just too exhausting, and now he began to wonder just how much longer he might have to live.

Despite the fact that he felt the end of his life was imminent, this was not a gloomy time for Jack. He declared it to be a happy period in his life. Joy's death had made heaven all the more real to him, and he was content to be coming to the end of his life. "Yes, autumn is really the best of the seasons," he wrote to a friend. "And I'm not sure that old age isn't the best part of life. But, of course, like autumn it doesn't last."

It seemed that while everyone was bracing himself for Jack's death, it was not yet his time to go. After three weeks in the hospital, Jack was well enough to return to The Kilns, where a male nurse looked after him while Walter did his best to manage Jack's affairs.

When Jack had been hospitalized, Warren was away vacationing in Ireland. When he had not returned to The Kilns by mid-August, Jack's friend George Sayer went to Ireland to retrieve him. But Warren would not come back. He said that he could not face watching Jack's health decline.

As September and the time of Walter's departure for the United States approached, Warren gathered up his courage and finally returned to The Kilns, ready to help look after his brother. Jack was glad to have him back and settled into a pleasant routine of resting, reading, entertaining visitors, and drinking endless cups of tea with Warren. Warren helped Jack write letters and put his affairs in order.

During October, as the trees lost their leaves, Jack began to lose his grip on life. Warren, who had feared his brother's end so much, wrote in his journal, "Yet those last weeks were not unhappy ones. Joy had left us, and once more as in bygone days we had no one but each other to turn to for comfort. The wheel had come full circle. Again we were together in a new 'little end room,' shutting out from our talk the ever present knowledge that the holidays were ending, and a new term fraught with unknown possibilities awaited us both."

Meanwhile, old faces began to reappear in Jack's life. In November, J. R. R. Tolkien came to visit Jack, though understandably their meeting was strained.

On Friday, November 22, 1963, the end finally came. Jack was calm and in little pain when he retired to his bed for an afternoon nap. At 5:30 Warren heard a thud and went to see what had happened. He found Jack lying on the floor, unconscious. Warren rushed to his side, but a few minutes later his brother slipped away. His kidneys had finally failed.

Surprisingly, the master storyteller's death was overshadowed by another death that captivated the world that day. Thousands of miles away from Oxford, across the Atlantic Ocean in Dallas, Texas, the president of the United States, John F. Kennedy, was assassinated as he made his way through the city's streets in a motorcade.

In keeping with what his brother would have wanted, Warren requested that Jack's funeral be for close friends and family only. Maureen Moore and David and Douglas Gresham followed the coffin out of Headington Quarry Church and into the adjoining graveyard, where C. S. Lewis was buried. It was November 26, 1963, three days before what would have been Jack's sixty-fifth birthday.

The seventh book of The Chronicles of Narnia, *The Last Battle,* ends with a scene in which Lucy Pevensie confronts Aslan with the suspicion that she and her parents are dead. Aslan replies, "Your father and mother and all of you are—as you used to call it in the Shadowlands—dead. The term is over: the holidays have begun. The dream is ended: this is the morning."

Jack concluded the book with the lines "All their life in this world and all their adventures in Narnia had only been the cover and the title page: now at last they were beginning Chapter One of the Great Story which no one on earth has read: which goes on for ever: in which every chapter is better than the one before."

Note to Readers

The narrative style of *C. S. Lewis: Master Storyteller* differs from that of other Christian Heroes: Then & Now biographies in regard to point of view. Normally the biographies are written from the subject's perspective, giving readers a focused slice of history from one person's viewpoint. *C. S. Lewis* is written from a broader angle, using an omniscient narrator. This wider perspective allowed the authors to showcase the rich historical context of Lewis's life and writings in a way that wouldn't have been possible in a narrative limited to Lewis's point of view.

In all other aspects, *C. S. Lewis: Master Storyteller* employs the same familiar storytelling style readers enjoy in the Christian Heroes: Then & Now series.

—The Publisher

Beahm, George. *Passport to Narnia: A Newcomer's Guide*. Hampton Roads Publishing Company, 2005.

Gormley, Beatrice. *C. S. Lewis: Christian and Storyteller*. Eerdmans Books for Young Readers, 1998.

Green, Roger Lancelyn, and Walter Hooper. *C. S. Lewis: A Biography*. Harcourt Brace Jovanovich, 1974.

Gresham, Douglas. *Jack's Life*. Broadman & Holman Publisher, 2005.

Hooper, Walter, ed. *All My Road Before Me: The Diary of C. S. Lewis 1922–1927*. Harcourt Brace Jovanovich, 1991.

Jacobs, Alan. *The Narnian: The Life and Imagination of C. S. Lewis*. HarperSanFrancisco, 2005.

Kilby, Clyde S., and Marjorie Lamp Mead, eds. *Brothers & Friends: The Diaries of Major Warren Hamilton Lewis*. Harper & Row, 1982.

Lewis, C. S. *Surprised by Joy*. Collins, 1959.

Lewis, W. H., ed. *Letters of C. S. Lewis*. Harcourt, Brace & World, 1966.

Sayer, George. *Jack: C. S. Lewis and His Times*. Harper & Row, 1988.

Wilson, A. N. *C. S. Lewis: A Biography*. W. W. Norton & Company, 1990.